Herbal Celebrations Cookbook

Herbal Celebrations Cookbook

Noël Richardson &
Jenny Cameron

Whitecap Books
Vancouver/Toronto

Whitecap Books
Vancouver/Toronto

Edited by Elaine Jones
Proofread by Elizabeth McLean
Cover design by Tanya Lloyd
Interior design by Hermani and Sorrentino Design
Cover photograph by Andrew Yeoman

Printed and bound in Canada

CANADIAN CATALOGUING IN PUBLICATION DATA

Richardson, Noël, 1937–

   Herbal celebrations cookbook

   Includes index.
   ISBN 1-55110-835-6

   1. Cookery (Herbs) 2. Farm life--British Columbia--Vancouver
Island. I. Cameron, Jenny. II. Title.
TX819.H4R52 2000   641.6'57   C00-910070-9

The publisher acknowledges the support of the Canada Council for the Arts and the Cultural Services Branch of the Government of British Columbia for our publishing program. We acknowledge the financial support of the Government of Canada through the Book Industry Development Program for our publishing activities.

To Andrew Yeoman, my herbal companion. Your chaise lounge communist appreciates all your work and support in the past 22 years.

Also I would like to thank all the great cookbook writers who have provided me in the last 40 years with a correspondence course for life in the kitchen.

—Noël Richardson

To David Crone, my husband, for his constant encouragement and love of my food.

To Noël Richardson, my mom, for her infinite love and support, without which I would not exist.

And to Andrew Yeoman for his patience and support over the last 20 years.

—Jenny Cameron

Acknowledgements

Appreciation and thanks to Sylvia Weinstock for her careful and fast word-processing, editing and expansive knowledge of food and culinary herbs. Thanks to Elaine Jones for her careful and sensitive editing and Krystyna Jones for her loving care of Nina which allowed the book to be written.

Contents

July and August

September and October

November and December

Introduction

A FEW YEARS AGO my daughter Jenny and I had a conversation about the various herbal cooking classes we had given in the past, and the dinners we had cooked for family and friends at Ravenhill Farm over the past 20 years. Some meals have faded in our culinary memories, but others found a place and have become part of our cooking traditions. Each time we repeated the menus the pleasure increased, and the idea of creating a book out of these experiences slowly jelled.

We moved to Ravenhill when Jenny was 15. After she left home, she went to college and professional cooking school, and traveled in Australia, New Zealand, England, Europe, India and Thailand. She returned to Victoria after a decade, and we began to do herbal cooking classes together in our big sunny yellow kitchen at the farm.

I found it a physical relief to have lots of young energy, and was delighted to hear the cooking inspirations Jenny had gleaned from her travels. At first we warily circled around the island in my kitchen, trying not to be bossy with each other. I had the wisdom of age and experience, plus years of being a home cook, and Jenny had professional training and a youthful, eclectic approach to food honed by her travels. I gave up being queen of the kitchen and found out how much more help you get when you resign from queendom. We both discovered what fun it was cooking together. I could be the storyteller, and she could keep chopping because she was young and her energy level was high. People who came to our classes seemed to like seeing a mother and daughter working together in an amiable, relaxed way.

From these classes emerged a stack of menus and recipes. We put on a grilling party where we grilled the whole meal—bread, vegetables, butterflied leg of lamb—everything but dessert. A French picnic on a sunny August day in the garden was wonderful: all the food smelled of freshly harvested garlic, basil and Provence. We had bread classes with bowls of dough all over the kitchen, each bowl at a different stage of development. We added herbs, sun-dried tomatoes and spicy Italian sausage to the bread, which made a robust lunch with a glass of good red wine. A traditional English dinner with roast goose and treacle tart took lots of research and was a refreshing change from turkey. My husband, Andrew, grew the herbs and vegetables and was always an excellent consultant and taster.

Sometimes we hit the road and did classes in Mill Bay, Vancouver and Calgary. Besides teaching classes, we cooked for families and friends. We made Easter dinners with our own lamb, a first of July barbecue to celebrate Canada's birthday and the anniversary of our arrival on the farm, now over 20 years ago. I look back over those two decades of cooking, gardening and living and remember the faces of family and friends sitting around the long dining room table enjoying food, wine and each other's company. I have been very lucky to land in such a place in midlife, and it makes me happy to see the next generation here, helping us cook and garden.

Four Japanese students came to stay one year and cooked Japanese food for us. They also taught us a beautiful grace which covers all bases. Before each meal they bowed their heads and gave thanks to the fisherman, the farmer and the cook. I have added the dishwasher to that list.

We realized that the theme of our book should be family, friends and celebrations around the table. The celebrations have evolved out of our lives and are deeply influenced and inspired by the garden at Ravenhill. Andrew grows so many wonderful things to cook with and also has a keen diner's appreciation of what he eats. He often spurs me to action by asking what I want from the garden. Or he'll offer to chop something in preparation for dinner, such as shallots or garlic. If I am very slow to respond, he suggests we order in pizza, which is the jolt I need to drop my book, get off the couch and go into the kitchen. On busy days we have been known to order in a pizza, but we cover it with fresh chopped basil and oregano, which truly transforms mundane food. Sometimes in the summer we take the two dogs and this herbed-up pizza out in our rowboat and drift about, munching happily.

Cooking for friends and family and breaking bread with them is the highest compliment you can pay them. Breaking bread is a form of social glue that creates societal and friendship bonds.

Celebration meals also relieve the tedium and boredom of daily life. Planning can fill your thoughts for hours and give you a spark of energy. I clean up the house and put the extra books and magazines into the back hall, a place where no one goes, for it is both the back stage and prop room for our lives.

Celebrations mark the year like signposts and help create layered memories that enrich our lives. It's interesting to think about how new traditions came about. One year we had Christmas in England, and on Christmas Eve we went to a cousin's house for dinner. The house was a converted oast house—those great round barns made of brick and timber used to dry hops—and parts of it dated back to the 13th-century. We walked to the village of Chiddingstone (where parts of *A Room With a View* were filmed) for the carol service in the 14th-century church. We returned to the oast house, and did we get solid English food? No. Jeanne, my cousin's wife, had spent much time in Norway and we had a Scandinavian dinner of fresh prawns, dark bread and beer. For dessert there was a traditional rice pudding with an almond in it. The meal was a simple, light, delicious prelude to Christmas dinner the next day. I came home to the farm determined to create my own version of this delightful Christmas Eve dinner, with British Columbia influences.

A visit to the Satellite Fish Store on the Sidney dock provided me with fresh oysters, smoked salmon and hand-peeled shrimp from Tofino. A couple of little pots of caviar, some black German bread, sour cream and lemons finished the menu. The first year, Andrew got out my Jewish-Russian cookbook and made real blinis with three yeast risings. They were as light as angel's wings, and were the perfect elegant touch. Champagne is served with this meal, which is now our Christmas Eve tradition, new but firmly entrenched. The cook can conserve his or her energy for Christmas dinner. The dropping of old hoary traditions that do not suit our diets or digestions—puddings made with beef suet or food that is attached to bad memories (such as family fights)—are good things to dispense with.

Feasts and celebration dinners also mark the seasons of the year. The arrival in the garden of asparagus, artichokes, strawberries and raspberries are all good excuses to cook and dine with friends and family. One year we held a family reunion to celebrate my grandfather's arrival in B.C. in 1886. He was 16 when he went to Saturna Island to start living the farming life. We barbecued a whole lamb we had raised and fed 60 of my grandfather's descendants. Their ages ranged from 2 to 85. The sun shone, and the 20-somethings had tents in the field. The lawn was covered with picnic tables. The wasps attacked the lamb as it cooked, but it kept them from bothering people. Jenny and Andrew basted the beast with brushes made of rose-mary dipped in olive oil, chopped garlic and oregano. The lamb, which took four hours to cook, was tender, delectable and easy to carve. I found the general directions for barbecuing the lamb in Madame Benoit's lamb cookbook.

Some people wonder why more and more cookbooks continue to be published. Barbara Haber, in an essay called "Follow The Food," says that looking closely at the collective and individual food habits of people can reveal them in new and unexpected ways, can be a shortcut for under-standing people's deepest and most hidden truths. Universities now gather culinary collections that people can study to gain important social, psycho-logical and historic insights. I have a collection of B.C. cookbooks written by various women's organizations, such as churches, schools and fire departments. To get an insight into a poor family's Depression-era meal, check out a recipe for supper composed of cold oatmeal from breakfast, fried in bacon grease, and served with sugar cane syrup. If one had no money to go to the grocery store this meal—breakfast re-framed—would have to do.

Jenny and I have compiled a series of menus and recipes that can be used throughout the year. There are two distinct voices in this book. It is a mother-daughter conversation with the reader. My voice is in the essays that appear before each season of menus. Jenny's voice is in the menus and recipes. As well, Andrew's gardening tips on growing herbs and vegetables appear throughout.

Cooks who read cookbooks do so for many reasons. I read for inspiration, for fantasy food, and to help me fall asleep. The nightly news is not conducive to a good, peaceful sleep, but reading a cookbook is. Do not feel you need to use these menus slavishly in their entirety. Take one recipe out of a menu and use it. Switch recipes around, or edit and combine the menus. This book is a slice of life from Ravenhill Farm. We hope it amuses, comforts and nourishes you. Remember, when all else fails, you can think of what you will have for dinner. This is one of life's truly dependable pleasures.

—Noël Richardson,
Ravenhill Farm

January
and
February

Comfort and Company:
Food for Frost Time

Man is the only animal that remains on friendly terms with the victims he intends to eat until he eats them.
—SAMUEL BUTLER

Strange to see how a good dinner and feasting reconciles everybody.
—SAMUEL PEPYS

Eating food with a knife and fork is like making love through an interpreter.
—ANON.

IN JANUARY AND FEBRUARY the gray coastal winter socks in and we all need help in counteracting the winter gloom. At first, suffering from post-Christmas blahs, I do little in the food department. After a couple of weeks spent mulling over gloomy thoughts, the sturdier part of my character stirs and demands action. You need company, it cries, some delicious food, and music, and a glowing fire in the fireplace.

I start telephoning friends and family, and the end result is often a potluck supper. Potluck suppers are often maligned as unsophisticated, low-class collections of boring casseroles. Or not enough food. Or seven desserts and no main course. I think potlucks have been given bad press. A good potluck creates a real sense of community and can be a collection of delicious food.

One way to guarantee good food is to choose friends who are very good cooks willing to go that extra mile for an occasion, not merely stopping to pick up some hummus, pita and diet soft drinks on their way to the party. My friends, Lynne and Dotter, and I have been doing ethnic potlucks for several years. We pick a theme–Japanese or Thai–or perhaps the last place one of us has traveled. Each of us cooks part of the meal. We decorate the table appropriately, light lots of candles, deck the house with fruit and flowers and have a wonderful evening. There is often a child or two, and partners, and we tell stories and discuss travel, books and movies. As we are all busy writers, artists, gardeners, farmers and teachers, none of us would have the time to put on such an evening by ourselves, and this is a much happier solution. The enticing thing about potlucks is that you only have to make one or two things, and the rest of the afternoon you can curl up with a book or take a walk in the afternoon before the guests come. The very casualness of it all is cheering, and you do not have to worry if the napkins match. Fussing is eliminated and duties shared. Martyrs in the kitchen make crotchety dinner companions.

However, sometimes I enjoy spending an entire gray winter day cooking for friends. It can be an intense, deeply happy occupation. I clear the decks, gather my ingredients, put on some good cooking music to keep me moving, and dig in. Josie, the stray Lab, loiters at my feet and gobbles up anything I drop. Andrew brings me herbs and greens from the garden to encourage me and chops precise, neat piles of shallots and garlic ready for the sauté pan.

I wonder about this primeval urge to gather family and friends around our table. What pleasure does it bring me? Am I doing it for love, praise, the sensual pleasure of cooking, chopping, stirring and tasting? Or is it a mixture of those two great motivators—greed and hunger—that brings us to the table? There is no simple answer to this complex question. When M.F.K. Fisher was asked why she wrote about food instead of power and love she answered, "It seems to me our three basic needs, for food, security, and love are so mixed and mingled and entwined that we cannot straightly think of one without the others. So it happens when I write about hunger I am really writing about life and the hunger for it, and the warmth and the love of it and the hunger for it ... and then the warmth and richness and the fine reality of hunger satisfied ... and it is all one."

The pleasures of January are sparse. With less warmth, less visual stimulation from the garden, it becomes important to focus on smaller, more subtle pleasures. In January and early February a few crocuses, snowdrops and yellow aconites are up. January needs yellow things. The flowering winter jasmine that crawls over an old shed sends out a stab of yellow that pierces the gray gloom.

The verdant green of spring and the heat of summer are absent, but there are other things that lift the spirits, like the view from our dining room window. We can see Hagan Creek, named after an early pioneer who built a log cabin there in the late 1850s. By January the trumpeter swans have begun to fly up the valley. They noisily flump down in the pond made by the flooding creek that divides the valley and runs out to sea. The arrival of the swans gives me a quick spurt of pleasure. The view from the kitchen window is of the upper meadow. The ewes are pregnant, and they huff and puff large steamy clouds of air. When I go near the fence, they gallop laboriously towards me, but it is purely cupboard love. I am the carrot lady to them. When I enter the field, they push against me and sniff my pockets, searching for more carrots.

In a west coast garden the cook can still grub around and find a few enticing flavors, depending on the mildness of the winter, and the auspicious use of cold frames. We usually have tough little romaine lettuces, arugula and parsley, all planted in late summer. I can find sorrel leaves and add their lemony sharpness to soups and salads.

Rosemary, sage, thyme and winter savory are perennial stalwarts all winter long. They keep their leaves, unlike tarragon and chives, which disappear in November for an underground winter holiday. When I tuck these friends of the cook under a leg of lamb, the bed of rosemary, thyme and bay leaves perfumes the meat, the pan juices, and the kitchen. There is always self-seeded kale, a generous plant that survives in any weather. A Dutch friend told me that as a child during the war in Europe she was sent to search for kale in empty lots so her mother could make a simple soup of kale and water. This sturdy plant fed many people during those difficult times. A healthy winter soup of kale can become quite glamorous with the addition of chicken stock, sour cream and garlic. Like turnips, kale needs a little glitz because it is such a sensible utilitarian vegetable.

The two menus for January and February are an eclectic appetizer party, and a homey Saturday night supper. They need not be potluck, though it would be fun to have two or three people cooking in the kitchen. The strong Asian flavors in the appetizer menu come naturally to West Coasters. My children were absorbing Asian flavors in the womb. Every B.C. town has a Chinese restaurant as a heritage from the 19th century when Chinese laborers were imported to work on the railways. The dishes have a fresh clean taste, and use lots of cilantro, which you can always buy in the markets even in the dead of winter. Place the appetizers on your prettiest plates with greenery such as lettuce, spinach and cabbage leaves. Serve with sake, cold beer, champagne or green tea. There is more to appetizers than sausage rolls and quiche. A buffet spread with carrot cilantro pâté, mixed green salad with nori avocado cones, a Chinese version of the Italian gremolada, soba noodle salad with pickled vegetables and watercress, and spicy chicken dumplings with ginger, garlic and cilantro sauce is a gift to your taste buds that will definitely spark up a winter evening.

About Using Fresh Herbs

At Ravenhill Farm we have an extraordinary abundance and variety of fresh herbs throughout the summer and a good staple supply of hardy herbs even in the winter months. Partly because of this, we are lavish in our use of herbs. Most people, even those who use a lot of herbs in their cooking, probably have a more modest herb garden.

When it comes to measuring the amounts specified in these recipes, keep in mind that herbs can vary in flavor and strength among varieties of the same herb. So use your own judgment when it comes to measuring; the quantities given are guidelines and the amount you use is strictly personal taste.

The Saturday night supper menu gives you a choice of rigatoni with spicy pork sausage, winter savory and portobello mushrooms, or the more complex osso buco, made with lamb shanks and rosemary. This is truly a rich and nourishing winter dish. For dessert there is a famous flourless chocolate cake Jenny learned to make when she worked at Deep Cove Chalet in Sidney after cooking school.

Frances Moore Lappé wrote that the act of putting in your mouth what the earth has grown is perhaps the most direct interaction with the earth. A thought for pondering on a winter evening.

Frost Fusion Feast

Why not host an Asian potluck dinner to brighten the gloomy month of January? Each guest can make part of the menu and the evening will give your spirits—and taste buds—a lift.

Carrot Cilantro Pâté

Smoked Salmon and Arugula Roll-ups

Mixed Greens, Nori Rolled Avocado and Warm Mushrooms
with a Sesame Vinaigrette

Spicy Chicken Dumplings in Soup

Sage and Rosemary Turkey Meatballs
with Cranberry Jalapeño Chutney

Caramelized Onion Bruschetta
with Fresh Sage and Italian Parsley

Warm Spinach Sauté with Sesame Vinaigrette

Soba Noodle Salad with Pickled Vegetables and Watercress

Carrot Cilantro Pâté

While staying with some vegan friends in England, I used to liberally spread a more conservative version of this pâté on my morning toast. It's a great alternative to the old standby, hummus. The cooked garlic gives it a wonderfully nutty flavor. It will keep for up to 2 weeks in a sealed jar in the refrigerator.

Makes approximately 1–1½ cups (240–360 mL)

> 2 Tbsp. (30 mL) olive oil
> 4–5 large cloves garlic, peeled
> 2 Tbsp. (30 mL) water
> ¼ bunch fresh cilantro
> Salt and freshly ground black pepper, to taste
> 3–4 medium carrots, coarsely chopped and simmered until tender
> ¼ cup (60 mL) cooked brown rice
> ¼ cup (60 mL) chickpeas
> 1 Tbsp. (15 mL) marmite
> Juice of ½ lemon
> ¼ cup (60 mL) extra virgin olive oil

Heat a small frying pan over medium heat. Add the oil and garlic and sauté for 5 minutes. Add the water, cover, turn down the heat and cook for another 5–6 minutes, until the garlic is soft.

Process the garlic, cilantro, salt and pepper in a food processor. Add the carrots, rice, chickpeas, marmite and lemon juice and process until smooth. Slowly drizzle in the olive oil while the motor is running. Taste for seasoning. Serve with crostini or fresh French bread.

Smoked Salmon and Arugula Roll-ups

I got the inspiration for this recipe when I worked for a catering company. The roll-ups are simple to make and a guaranteed crowd-pleaser. The flavor of arugula blends beautifully with the other ingredients, but you can substitute a head of red or green leaf lettuce.

Makes 30–40 slices, depending on tortilla size

> 5 or 6 flour tortillas (try basil, sun-dried tomato or whole wheat)
> 9 oz. (255 g) cream cheese
> 2 bunches arugula, washed and dried
> 6 sorrel leaves, julienned
> 1 lb. (455 g) thinly sliced smoked salmon
> 1 medium red onion, cut in half and thinly sliced
> ½ cup (120 mL) capers
> Juice of 1 lemon
> Freshly ground black pepper, to taste

Lay a tortilla on a clean countertop or large cutting board. Spread cream cheese in a thin, smooth layer, covering the entire tortilla. Place some arugula across the center, enough to touch both sides. Sprinkle some sorrel on top. Add a layer of smoked salmon. Place some onion slices over top. Sprinkle with approximately 1 tsp. (5 mL) capers, and ½ tsp. (2.5 mL) lemon juice. Season with black pepper.

Rolling away from you, roll the tortilla up snugly, but gently. Repeat with the remaining tortillas, wrapping each one in plastic wrap when completed. Refrigerate the rolls. Just before serving, cut each roll on a slight diagonal into approximately ½ inch (1.2 cm) slices. Arrange the slices on a platter in a circular pattern, layering the sections on top of each other.

Arugula

It can be sown in late February under a cold frame or outside in March. The young shoots are a taste sensation when only 2 or 3 inches (5 to 7.5 cm) high. Late spring and summer sowings are best made under a floating row cover, which keeps the leaves mild and tender. Seeds are easily collected from mature plants.

'Rustica', a perennial arugula, has narrower, tougher leaves and a stronger flavor. Chopped coarsely, it really spices up a take-out pizza.

Mixed Greens, Nori Rolled Avocado and Warm Mushrooms with a Sesame Vinaigrette

I created this salad while making sushi and salad at the same time. The result was fantastic. This recipe is versatile and very popular. The nori (dried roasted seaweed) is available at Asian stores and most large food markets.

Serves 4–6

> 1 avocado, just ripe
> 2 sheets nori
> ½ lb. (225 g) brown and/or wild mushrooms (such as portobello, shiitake, oyster)
> 2 Tbsp. (30 mL) olive oil
> Salt and freshly ground black pepper, to taste
> Approximately 4–5 cups (950 mL–1.2 L) mixed greens (such as spinach, arugula, watercress, radicchio, Belgian endive, winter kale, sorrel)
> 4–5 radishes, sliced
> 1 recipe Sesame Vinaigrette (see page 17)
> 1 tsp. (5 mL) black sesame seeds, for garnish

Slice the avocado into 8 equal pieces. Cut each sheet of nori into 4 squares. Place an avocado slice in one corner of a nori square and roll it up like a cone. Repeat with the remaining nori and avocado.

Sauté the mushrooms in the olive oil for approximately 5 minutes. Season with salt and pepper. Arrange the greens and radishes on a platter. Place the avocado cones so they rise up out of the salad. Spoon the warm mushrooms on top. Drizzle the vinaigrette over everything. Sprinkle with a few sesame seeds, and serve immediately.

Sesame Vinaigrette

Makes approximately 1¼ cups (300 mL)

>   2 large cloves garlic
>   ¼ cup (60 mL) finely chopped fresh cilantro
>   ¼ cup (60 mL) finely chopped fresh chives
>   1 generous Tbsp. (15 mL) Dijon mustard
>   ¼ cup (60 mL) rice wine vinegar
>   1 Tbsp. (15 mL) soy sauce
>   ⅔–1 cup (160–240 mL) olive oil
>   ¼ cup (60 mL) toasted sesame seeds
>   Salt and freshly ground black pepper, to taste

Purée the garlic in a food processor. Add the cilantro, chives, mustard, vinegar and soy sauce. Process until smooth. With the motor running, slowly add the olive oil until smooth. Add the sesame seeds and pulse until mixed. Season with salt and pepper.

Spicy Chicken Dumplings in Soup

My sister and I are huge fans of dim sum. She kept encouraging me to try our own at home, and when I did, these dumplings soon became a family favorite. I encourage you to play with the chicken mixture, adding other ingredients such as shiitake mushrooms, water chestnuts and bamboo shoots. Gyoza wrappers and sambal oelek, a chili pepper condiment, can be found in Asian food markets. Sambal oelek can also be found in most large food markets.

Serves 8

        6 or more cloves garlic, peeled and sliced
        ½ Tbsp. (7.5 mL) olive oil
        5–6 cups (1.2–1.5 L) hot chicken stock
        ½–¾ lb. (225–340 g) ground chicken or turkey
        1 cup (240 mL) cilantro, finely chopped
        1 Tbsp. (15 mL) sesame oil
        2 Tbsp. (30 mL) soy sauce
        ¼ cup (60 mL) freshly grated Parmesan cheese
        1 small onion, finely chopped and lightly sautéed
        1 Tbsp. (15 mL) sambal oelek
        1 16-oz. (455-g) package wonton or gyoza wrappers
        2 green onions, finely chopped
        Juice of 1 lime
        Salt and black pepper, to taste

Sauté the garlic slivers in the olive oil until blonde and a little crispy, and add to the hot chicken stock. Keep the broth warm while you prepare the dumplings.

Combine the chicken or turkey, half the cilantro, the sesame oil, soy sauce, Parmesan cheese, onion and sambal oelek. Mix well. Lay 3–4 wonton or gyoza wrappers out, and place a generous teaspoonful of chicken mixture in the center of each one. Bring up all 4 sides, and pinch gently around the top until the dumpling is sealed. Repeat with the remaining filling and wrappers. (You won't need the whole package for this recipe. The rest of the wrappers can be frozen.)

Bring a pot of water to a boil and gently add the dumplings. Simmer approximately 4 minutes, until some float to the surface. With a slotted spoon, remove the dumplings from the simmering water.

Place the dumplings in the hot chicken broth. Add the green onion, lime juice and the remaining cilantro. Adjust seasoning before serving.

Ginger Garlic Sauce

Here is another way to serve the dumplings. Instead of serving them in soup, once the dumplings have been cooked in the above recipe, toss them in this tangy ginger garlic sauce.

Serves 4–6

> 2 tsp. (10 mL) finely minced ginger
> 2 large cloves garlic, minced
> 2 Tbsp. (30 mL) minced chives or green onions
> 2 Tbsp. (30 mL) minced cilantro or fresh tarragon
> 3 Tbsp. (45 mL) lemon or lime juice
> 3 Tbsp. (45 mL) unseasoned rice wine vinegar
> 2 Tbsp. (30 mL) light soy sauce
> ½ tsp. (2.5 mL) salt
> ½ tsp. (2.5 mL) sambal oelek
> 1 Tbsp. (15 mL) sugar
> 2 tsp. (10 mL) cornstarch

Combine all the ingredients in a small saucepan and mix well. Bring the sauce to a simmer. Cook until the sauce is slightly thickened. Toss the cooked dumplings in the sauce. Serve immediately.

Horseradish

European horseradish has a cluster of massive roots which can be extracted singly without destroying the parent. Given moist, deep soil, horseradish can be invasive; we grow it in a half-barrel, which may add an antique oak and whisky flavor.

Japanese wasabi is a different species from European horseradish, but it has a somewhat similar flavor and two-year-old roots are very pungent when freshly grated. Wasabi grows wild by mountain streams, but it is said to succeed in gardens.

Sage and Rosemary Turkey Meatballs
with Cranberry Jalapeño Chutney

These meatballs suit the winter mood. They are lower in fat and a nice change from beef. Serve them with your favorite pasta sauce as an alternative to ground meat. You can freeze the meatballs uncooked. Thaw them before cooking.

Makes 35–40

> 1½ lbs. (680 g) fresh raw ground turkey
> ⅔ cup (160 mL) fine bread crumbs
> 1 egg, beaten
> 3 Tbsp. (45 mL) finely chopped green onion or chives
> 1 Tbsp. (15 mL) finely chopped fresh sage and rosemary combined
> 1 Tbsp. (15 mL) horseradish
> 4 shallots, peeled and finely chopped
> 1 Tbsp. (15 mL) tamari soy sauce (or other dark soy sauce)
> Freshly ground black pepper and salt, to taste

Combine all the ingredients in a bowl and mix well. Form into cocktail-size meatballs and bake in a 350°F (175°C) oven for 20–30 minutes until done. Serve with Cranberry Jalapeño Chutney.

Cranberry Jalapeño Chutney

A spicy, sweet homemade chutney to accompany different meat dishes. It will keep at least 2 weeks in the refrigerator, or it can be frozen.

Makes approximately 1–1½ cups (240–360 mL)

> 1 12-oz. (340-g) package fresh or frozen cranberries
> 1 jalapeño pepper, seeded and finely chopped
> 2 tsp. (10 mL) freshly grated ginger
> Zest of 1 orange
> Juice of ½ orange
> ½ cup (120 mL) honey

⅓ cup (80 mL) white wine vinegar
¼ tsp. (1.2 mL) allspice
Salt and freshly ground black pepper, to taste

Combine all the ingredients in a saucepan and bring to a boil. Simmer gently for 10–12 minutes. Let cool and refrigerate until serving.

Caramelized Onion Bruschetta with Fresh Sage and Italian Parsley

There are many things one could have on a slice of toasted baguette. Traditionally, in Italy, you would simply rub a cut garlic clove on toasted bread drizzled with a little good olive oil. This dish is a little richer, and very comforting to eat when you have the January blues. Try it with a glass of Shiraz or Cabernet.

Makes approximately 20 pieces

2 Tbsp. (30 mL) olive oil
6 medium yellow onions, cut in half and thinly sliced
¼ cup (60 mL) port or robust red wine
1 Tbsp. (15 mL) balsamic or red wine vinegar
1 tsp. (5 mL) sugar
Salt and freshly ground black pepper, to taste
1 Tbsp. (15 mL) finely chopped fresh sage
1 baguette, sliced approximately ½ inch (1.2 cm) thick, at a slight angle
3 cloves garlic, pressed and mixed with ¼ cup (60 mL) extra virgin olive oil
¼ cup (60 mL) finely chopped fresh parsley, for garnish
1 Tbsp. (15 mL) finely chopped chives, for garnish

(directions over page)

Heat the olive oil in a large frying pan over medium heat. Add the onions and sauté until soft. Add the vinegar, port or wine, sugar, salt, pepper and sage. Sauté for approximately 30 minutes over medium heat, stirring occasionally, until the mixture is a dark golden brown. While the onions are cooking, place the sliced bread on a cookie sheet and brush with the garlic oil. Toast lightly in a 300°F (150°C) oven for approximately 10 minutes. When the onions are done, place a small bunch on each toast, and decorate with parsley and chives.

Warm Spinach Sauté with Sesame Vinaigrette

Most Japanese restaurants serve ice-cold spinach with sesame seeds. This tasty dish is beneficial when you are low in iron. My version is served warm or at room temperature. Winter kale is a delicious substitute for the spinach.

Serves 4–6

  1 Tbsp. (15 mL) olive oil
  2 shallots, minced
  2 bunches fresh spinach, well-washed and dried, stems removed
  1 recipe Sesame Vinaigrette (see page 17)
  1 Tbsp. (15 mL) finely chopped chives (optional)
  1 Tbsp. (15 mL) black sesame seeds (optional)

Heat the olive oil in a large frying pan or wok over medium heat. Add shallots and sauté for 2 minutes. Add the spinach and sauté until it's wilted, but still bright green. Transfer to a small platter and drizzle the Sesame Vinaigrette over top. Decorate with chives and black sesame seeds, if desired. To serve this as a canapé, mold the cooked spinach in an egg cup and invert it on a rice cracker. Spoon the vinaigrette over top of each cracker.

Soba Noodle Salad with Pickled Vegetables and Watercress

My mom and I love soba noodles, and often use them in a simple miso soup for lunch. This recipe is a refreshing combination of ingredients that creates a super winter salad. Soba noodles can be found in Asian markets and specialty food stores. Daikon radish is available in Asian markets and many large food stores. Save the pickling juice when you drain the vegetables—it's perfect for making sushi rice. (Pickled vegetables are also a deliciously crunchy, sweet and sour addition to maki rolls.)

Serves 4

For the pickled vegetables:

1½ cups (360 mL) unseasoned rice wine vinegar

½ cup (120 mL) sugar

2 Tbsp. (30 mL) sweet sherry or fortified wine (such as Marsala)

1 Tbsp. (15 mL) salt

2 medium carrots, finely julienned

1 medium daikon radish, finely julienned

1 red bell pepper, finely julienned

Combine the rice wine vinegar, sugar, sherry or wine, and salt in a small saucepan and simmer for 2–3 minutes until the sugar dissolves.

Combine the carrot, radish and pepper in a small bowl and pour the pickling juice over top, tossing well. Marinate at least 4 hours, or overnight, mixing occasionally.

Mint

Mint is a rampant runner in the garden, so we keep it contained in tubs. There is a new form of mint, 'Hillary's Sweet Lemon', which has a lot of potential in the kitchen.

For the dressing:

    1 Tbsp. (15 mL) fish sauce

    Juice and finely chopped zest of 1 lemon or lime

    2 Tbsp. (30 mL) sesame oil

    4 Tbsp. (60 mL) hoisin sauce

    2 Tbsp. (30 mL) finely chopped fresh cilantro

    1 Tbsp. (15 mL) finely chopped fresh mint
      (use extra cilantro if mint is unavailable)

    2 tsp. (10 mL) freshly grated ginger

    2 cloves garlic, finely chopped or pressed

    2 shallots, finely chopped

Combine all ingredients well, and set aside.

To make the salad:

    1 16-oz. (455-g) package Japanese soba noodles

    1 bunch watercress, woody stems removed, coarsely chopped

    2 green onions, finely chopped

    ½ lb. (225 g) hand-peeled shrimp (optional)

    5 or 6 cilantro sprigs

Drain the pickling juice from the vegetables and reserve, if desired.

Bring a medium to large pot of water to a gentle simmer. Drop the noodles in, and cook for approximately 5–8 minutes, until just barely tender. Drain, immerse in cold water until cool, and drain well. In a large shallow bowl combine the soba noodles, pickled vegetables, watercress, green onion and dressing. Toss well. Sprinkle with the shrimp and garnish with cilantro sprigs.

Saturday Night Supper

This savory supper will help battle post-Christmas blahs and cold, wet January nights. You'll soon find yourself singing, "Soup of the evening, beautiful soup." This menu offers a choice of main course dishes; both are hearty, aromatic dishes for a cold night.

Winter Greens with Warm Golden Garlic and Thyme Dressing

Provençal Garlic Soup with Rouille

Rigatoni with Spicy Pork Sausage, Winter Savory and Portobello Mushrooms

or

Osso Buco alla Milanese, Mint Gremolada and Champagne Lemon Risotto

Deep Cove Chalet Flourless Chocolate Cake

Winter Greens with Warm Golden Garlic and Thyme Dressing

A cheerful, warming winter salad.

Serves 4

> 7 oz. (200 g) each of 4 of your favorite greens (such as
> kale, sorrel, arugula, radicchio, frisée)
> 2 Tbsp. (30 mL) olive oil
> 6 shallots, peeled and sliced in half lengthwise
> 3 slices of your favorite bread, cut into croutons,
> approximately 1 inch (2.5 cm) square
> 2 Tbsp. (30 mL) olive oil
> 6 medium cloves garlic
> Salt and freshly ground black pepper, to taste
> 2 tsp. (10 mL) fresh thyme leaves
> ¼ cup (60 mL) fresh lemon juice
> 1 tsp. (5 mL) honey
> 1 Tbsp. (15 mL) grainy mustard
> ⅔ cup (160 mL) extra virgin olive oil

Chiffonade (thinly slice) the greens, and arrange them on a platter or in a large shallow bowl. Heat 2 Tbsp. (30 mL) olive oil over medium heat in a large frying pan. Add the shallots and sauté for 3 minutes. Remove the shallots, add the croutons, and lightly sauté for approximately 5 minutes, stirring every couple of minutes.

In a large frying pan, heat 2 Tbsp. (30 mL) olive oil over medium-low heat. Add the garlic cloves, salt and pepper and sauté until golden brown and tender, approximately 10 minutes. Place the garlic and thyme in a food processor, and purée until smooth. Add the lemon juice, honey and mustard, and blend. While the motor is running, slowly add the ⅔ cup (160 mL) olive oil until smooth. Taste for seasoning. Return the dressing to the frying pan, and warm it very gently, without boiling.

Scatter the shallots and croutons over the greens and drizzle the warm dressing over top. Serve immediately.

Provençal Garlic Soup with Rouille

This soup is also called *Aigo Bouida* (Garlic Broth), or "Save Your Life Soup."

Serves 4

For the rouille:

    4 cloves garlic
    ½ tsp. (2.5 mL) salt
    Freshly ground black pepper, to taste
    1 tsp. (5 mL) cayenne powder or hot sauce
    1 bunch fresh parsley, washed and dried, stems removed
    1 slice good white bread, sprinkled with 1 Tbsp. (15 mL) milk or water
    2 egg yolks
    ¼ cup (60 mL) bottled or canned pimento, or peeled, roasted
        red pepper
    ⅔ cup (160 mL) olive oil

Blend the garlic, salt, pepper and cayenne or hot sauce in a food processor. Add the parsley and blend. Add the bread, egg yolks, pimento or roasted pepper and olive oil. Process until combined and set aside.

For the soup:

    5 cups (1.2 L) chicken stock
    6 large cloves garlic
    Zest of ½ orange
    2 bay leaves
    5 fresh sage leaves
    2 sprigs fresh thyme
    ½ tsp. (2.5 mL) saffron threads
    ¼ cup (60 mL) freshly grated Parmesan cheese (optional)

Heat the chicken stock until it boils. Add the garlic, orange zest, bay leaves, sage, thyme and saffron. Simmer for 20 minutes. Strain. Add the rouille to the stock and serve immediately. Sprinkle Parmesan cheese on the soup, if desired.

Rigatoni with Spicy Pork Sausage, Winter Savory and Portobello Mushrooms

A meaty, peppery pasta dish with the sharp, clean taste of winter savory.

Serves 4

> 2 Tbsp. (30 mL) extra virgin olive oil
> 3 cloves garlic, finely chopped
> 3 medium portobello mushrooms, cut into eighths
> 2 Tbsp. (10 mL) finely chopped fresh winter savory
> Salt and freshly ground black pepper, to taste
> ½ cup (120 mL) red wine
> 1 28-oz. (796-mL) can whole Italian plum tomatoes
> 6 high-quality spicy pork sausages, cooked and cut into
>   bite-size pieces
> ½ tsp. (2.5 mL) chili flakes (optional)
> 1 lb. (455 g) rigatoni
> 1 cup (240 mL) freshly grated Parmesan or Romano cheese
> ½ cup (120 mL) finely chopped green onion or Welsh onion

In a large sauté pan, heat the oil over medium heat. Add the garlic and sauté for 2 minutes. Add the mushrooms and winter savory and season with salt and pepper. Sauté until the mushrooms are soft. Add the red wine and simmer for 2 minutes. Add the tomatoes, squashing them gently with a wooden spoon. If you want tomato chunks, just break them up a bit. Bring back to a simmer and add the sausage and chili flakes, if desired. Simmer gently for approximately 30 minutes.

While the sauce is simmering, bring a large pot of salted water to a boil. Cook the rigatoni until al dente, approximately 12–15 minutes. Drain, reserving a small amount of pasta water, about ¼ cup (60 mL). Return the rigatoni to the pot and toss with the water and a drizzle of olive oil, if desired, to keep the pasta from sticking. Divide the rigatoni among 4 bowls and spoon the sauce over top. Garnish with the grated cheese and chopped green onion.

Osso Buco alla Milanese

Throughout my cooking career, my passion for Italian cuisine has inspired me to attempt to master dishes such as Osso Buco alla Milanese. I must confess I prefer to make this dish with organic lamb shank as opposed to delicious, but—in many people's view—politically incorrect milk-fed veal. The literal translation of osso buco is "bone with a hole," so the choice of meat is a personal decision. This is a delicious alternative to the rigatoni for a main course. Serve it with Champagne Lemon Risotto and Mint Gremolada. You can ask your butcher to tie up the lamb shank pieces for you.

Serves 4

¼ cup (60 mL) butter
2 medium celery stalks, finely chopped
2 medium carrots, finely chopped
1 onion, finely chopped
3 cloves garlic, finely chopped
Zest of ¼ lemon
¼ cup (60 mL) olive oil
¾ cup (180 mL) all purpose flour
8 2-inch (5-cm) lamb shank pieces, tied with kitchen twine around
    the outside
1 cup (240 mL) dry white wine, or dry white vermouth
1½ cups (360 mL) meat stock
1 14-oz. (398-mL) can whole plum tomatoes, coarsely chopped
1 Tbsp. (15 mL) fresh thyme
6 fresh basil leaves
2 bay leaves
½ cup (120 mL) finely chopped Italian parsley
1 tsp. (5 mL) finely chopped fresh rosemary
Salt and freshly ground black pepper, to taste

(directions over page)

Preheat the oven to 350°F (175°C).

Place the butter, celery, carrot and onion in a large, heavy, oven-proof casserole that has a tight-fitting lid. Cook over medium heat for 10 minutes until the vegetables are soft. Add the garlic and lemon zest. Remove from the heat.

Heat the olive oil in a large frying pan over medium heat. Place the flour in a bowl and toss the shanks in the flour, shaking off the excess. Brown the shanks on all sides. Place them on top of the vegetables in the casserole.

Remove any excess fat from the frying pan and deglaze with the wine, simmering for 3 minutes. Add the stock and bring to a simmer. Add the tomatoes, thyme, basil, bay leaves, parsley, rosemary, salt and pepper. Pour the broth over the lamb. Return the casserole to the heat and bring back to a simmer. Cover tightly and place in the oven for approximately 2 hours, turning and basting the lamb every 20 minutes. The lamb is done when it seems very tender when pricked with a fork, and the sauce is thick and creamy.

Mint Gremolada

Traditionally, osso buco calls for a garnish of fresh herbs, lemon zest and finely chopped garlic known as gremolada. It may be served separately as a condiment or added to the shanks as they finish cooking. If fresh mint is unavailable, substitute fresh parsley for the mint.

Serves 4

> Zest of 2 lemons, finely minced
> 2 cloves garlic, finely minced
> ½ cup (120 mL) chopped fresh parsley
> 2 Tbsp. (30 mL) finely chopped mint

Mix all ingredients together. Serve with the osso buco.

About Gremolada

While researching new recipes for my cooking classes, I began creating different gremoladas for a variety of dishes, using particular herbs and zests to complement each dish. The chart below will help you choose herbs for different types of dishes. Chop them finely and combine them with zest, garlic and shallots.

	lemon zest	lime zest	shallots and garlic	mint	parsley	basil	tarragon	cilantro	chervil	rosemary
Asian	♦	♦	•	•		•		•		
East Indian		•	•	•						
French	•		•	•	•	•	•		•	
Italian	•		•		•	•	•			•
Lamb	•		•	•	•					•
Beef	♦♦		•		•	•		•		•
Game or Duck	♦♦		•	•	•	•	•			•
Chicken	•	•	•	•	•	•	•	•	•	•
Seafood	•	•				•	•	•	•	•

NOTE: ♦ add ginger
♦♦ use orange zest

Champagne Lemon Risotto

A simple, elegant, creamy companion for osso buco.

Serves 4–6

> 4–5 cups (950 mL–1.2 L) chicken stock
> ½ tsp. (2.5 mL) saffron threads
> 3 Tbsp. (45 mL) butter
> 2 cloves garlic, finely chopped
> 1 small onion, finely chopped
> 2 cups (475 mL) Arborio rice
> Juice of 1 lemon
> 1 cup (240 mL) dry champagne
> ½ cup (120 mL) Parmesan cheese

Heat the stock to a gentle simmer. Add the saffron. Melt the butter in a heavy saucepan and sauté the garlic and onion for 1 minute. Add the rice and sauté for another 2 minutes. Over a period of 18 minutes, add the stock, one ladle at a time, while stirring constantly. As the stock is absorbed, add another ladle. After approximately 15 minutes, add the lemon juice, champagne and Parmesan cheese. Continue cooking and stirring for another 3–5 minutes. Add more stock if necessary. The rice should be cooked al dente and be creamy but not watery.

For a basic risotto, omit the champagne, using extra stock instead.

Deep Cove Chalet Flourless Chocolate Cake

This cake is deliciously rich and decadent on its own, or it can be served with whipped cream on the side.

Serves 8–10

    1¼ cups (300 mL) butter
    16 oz. (455 g) good-quality, semi-sweet chocolate, dark or white
    10 eggs, separated
    1½ cups (360 mL) sugar

Preheat the oven to 250°F (120°C). Grease a 12-inch (30-cm) spring-form pan and dust it with flour.

In a double boiler, melt the butter and chocolate. While the chocolate is melting, whip the egg yolks with the sugar for approximately 10 minutes until creamy. Fold the chocolate mixture into the egg yolks. Whip the egg whites until stiff. Fold into the chocolate mixture. Fill the springform pan, and bake for 2 hours. Insert a toothpick in the cake. If it comes out dry, the cake is done.

Remove the cake from the oven and place it on a rack to cool. Open the springform and carefully remove the cake. You will note that the cake will sink, like a soufflé.

Serve warm or at room temperature with a light sprinkling of icing sugar.

March
and
April

The First Part of Spring: Primeval Urges

Oliver Twist had asked for more.

—CHARLES DICKENS

Use the butter knife. Do not wear curlers in your hair or a bathing suit to the table. Do not make personal remarks. Excessive gigglers eat in the kitchen.

—MY FATHER'S TABLE MANNER RULES

No mean woman can cook well. It calls for a light head, a generous spirit, and a large heart.

—PAUL GAUGUIN

WHEN MARCH AND APRIL come round I always feel this is the most exciting time of year for the cook and gardener. There is promise and hope everywhere—in the garden, in the cook and in the gardener's fantasies. "This year we will have" and "this year we will plant" are phrases that go through our heads. The grim reality of crop failure, insect attacks and bad weather are not really apparent until July.

Of course, when I am participating in other seasons, I always think they are the best and the most exciting: the heat of summer, the crispness of fall, and the excitement of winter and Christmas. Happily for me, I love whatever season I am in and forget that I loved the previous months better at the time.

In early spring I have a deep hunger for the newly sprouting green herbs. Tarragon and chives have leading roles in the garden and on my dinner plates. I pick bunches of chives and snip them into little Chinese bowls and put them on everything I eat. Cover a fried or poached egg with a handful, throw them into sandwiches, soups, salad dressings, marinades, fish, crab, oysters, mix them in butter to put on fresh bread or on toast with smoked salmon. The subtle onion taste adds a piquancy that spring food needs—a true herbal pick-me-up. Chives stimulate your taste buds and I think they improve your digestion, as well as make your food look very pretty. Throw away your puritan feelings about food. Herbs do make your food look more appealing, as well as having the more pragmatic virtues of adding vitamins and digestive qualities.

Easter and rebirth are themes of the first part of spring. To me, Easter, with all its egg symbols, is a Christian festival layered over ancient pagan fertility rites. All these symbols are intertwined and have become delightfully muddled over the centuries. Lamb, which we raise and always cook for Easter dinner, has Christian and pagan significance, as well as Greek overtones. The Easter dinner menu is redolent with garlic, bay leaves, lemons, chives, rosemary and olive oil. We include phyllo for another Greek touch, and I decorate the table with a collection of Ukrainian Easter eggs that my sister sends from Alberta.

Another menu is a spring lunch we have often done: large, organic, free-range chickens stuffed with tarragon and roasted. Sharp and licorice-flavored, raw tarragon has almost a toothpaste bite, but when cooked it becomes much more subtle on the tongue and a mellow companion for roast chicken.

Roast chicken was a favorite Sunday dinner for me as a child— much more exciting than roast beef. Cold leftover chicken was an added pleasure. It always made Monday lunches more exciting—better than Spam and mustard sandwiches. We raised chickens and my mother, being the tough independent Gulf Island girl she was, would go to the chicken pen, seize the victim, and proceed to the woodshed and chop off its head. Sometimes I watched this horror show with a mixture of excitement, fear and disgust. I know if I was left to kill animals I would not be able to, and would live on roots, seeds and berries.

My hens, "the girls," start to lay more as the hours of light increase. They also get atavistic urges to increase their kind and start laying in secret nests all over the barn and in the field. They will hide eggs in the loft (they know I won't climb the ladder), in old stored garden furniture, in the leaf mold pile and in the burn pile. Visiting children can be kept occupied for a long time searching, and then we have to perform the old test. We place the eggs in a large sink of water: the ones that float are too old to eat. Whether this rule is scientifically based I do not know, but it seems to work for us. I do not sell secret nest eggs in case a rotten one has slipped in.

Sometimes, for hostess gifts I make a little basket filled with clean yellow straw with brown eggs nested in it. The hostess often puts this basket on the table with her centerpiece.

Eggs have a certain charm and are one of my favorite foods. They are so simply shaped, such perfectly compact, clever containers and so full of flavor and nourishment. We once stayed with an elderly Danish actress in California. She was a great faded old beauty and ran an organic avocado farm. I loved her diet, which consisted of good bread and cheese, avocados and eggs—liberally washed down with California white wine. I am saving this diet for my eighties.

In April, the endives that Andrew carefully seeded last summer and nurtured in beds of sawdust all fall and winter poke their pointy heads through the sawdust. For several weeks, crisp, raw, steamed and braised endives become the number-one vegetable. Grown in the garden in rich compost, they are very sweet, not bitter like some endives you find in the market. Travel does not become vegetables.

For dessert in early spring there is rosy-pink rhubarb and sweet cicely. This lacy, ferny herb sweetens the rhubarb, and is also pretty in bouquets. It likes to live in a cool damp place with a little shade. Chervil is another ferny herb that likes damp shade, and seeds itself in strange places, such as under the old Douglas firs or in a pile of old dead plants. As soon as the hot sun comes it vanishes, to reappear in the cooler fall weather. Let it go to seed and you will have a spasmodic supply of chervil. One year we had a huge crop under the grape vines, mixed with feverfew. It was a beautiful sight and a horticultural surprise. Chervil is beloved by French chefs, and any sauce with eggs is the perfect match. It also has a licorice flavor. Why are so many herbs flavored with licorice or lemon? An interesting thought to ponder.

The other menu in the first part of spring is a Sunday brunch. Brunch is a relaxed easy way to entertain. We serve Bullshot, which is like a hot Bloody Mary soup that quickly warms up the company. Another favorite is fresh, just-squeezed orange juice with champagne. Suddenly the workaday world seems far away. I remember an old radical friend from the sixties whose motto—uttered as she quaffed champagne—was, "Nothing is too good for the working classes."

Jenny makes a huge garlic potato tortilla flavored with sorrel and chives. There is a bit of brunch theatre and gymnastics as she flips the giant omelet in the air and catches it perfectly. A Spanish friend called Paco taught her how to make it. He was an impressive garlic eater, and at 50 he could bicycle 50 miles (80 km) at a stretch. Homemade scones are also served. My theory is that if you serve homemade bread or scones, that is what they will remember.

This is a good time of year to make some tarragon vinegar, as tarragon is growing so profusely. Use a good white wine vinegar or rice

Purple Sprouting Broccoli

Seeds can be sown in April, May or June for eating in the early spring of the next year. If you allow an early strong plant to set seeds, you will have healthy plants the following year, and so on. A short-term loss for a longer-term gain.

wine vinegar. Wash the herb, bring the vinegar to a boil, fill sterilized bottles with vinegar and stuff the bottles with tarragon, using a chopstick. Sometimes I add a peeled shallot for a certain Frenchness.

Now is the time to plant lettuce seeds. Broad beans are up, having been planted in October along with garlic and shallots. We compost the artichokes and begin staring at the asparagus bed for early signs of those delicious tips. The purple sprouting broccoli is getting pickable. It was planted last year at midsummer, and is a pleasure in early spring when one longs for fresh greenery on the plate. A great pasta sauce combines the purple sprouting broccoli with chopped garlic, anchovies and some olive oil. The sharpness of the anchovies and the sweet broccoli taste perk up the palate and it only takes minutes to make. March and April are tantalizing, teasing months, for there are all these hints of garden pleasures to come in May and June.

Easy Easter Dinner
with Greek Dreams

Easter is a time of celebratory feasts in Greece. This dinner menu shows its Greek roots in the rich flavors of lamb, feta cheese, ouzo and, of course, plenty of spring herbs.

Tomato Feta Kisses with Oregano and Chives

Lemon Oregano Roast Leg of Lamb

Briam—Mixed Roasted Vegetables

Ouzo Orange Ice

Tomato Feta Kisses with Oregano and Chives

Everyone loves these kisses. This is a catering-size recipe that will satisfy a crowd. Serve them with a bowl of kalamata olives.

Makes 60 kisses

> ½ lb. (225 g) feta cheese, crumbled
> ½ cup (120 mL) sun-dried tomatoes in oil, finely chopped
> ¼ cup (60 mL) finely chopped chives
> ¼ cup (60 mL), finely chopped Greek oregano
> Salt and freshly ground black pepper, to taste
> 10 sheets phyllo dough
> ½ cup (120 mL) melted butter

Preheat the oven to 375°F (190°C).

Combine the cheese, tomatoes and herbs in a bowl and season with salt and pepper.

Place one sheet of phyllo dough horizontally in front of you, on a flat, dry surface. (Keep the remainder of the phyllo covered with a damp cloth to prevent drying out.) Brush the phyllo sheet lightly with butter, and then place another sheet on top. Brush lightly with butter. With a sharp knife, divide the sheets into 12 squares, 4 across and 3 down. Place approximately 1 tsp. (5 mL) of filling on each square. Gather up the sides of each square, and pinch gently round the middle until secured. Repeat until all the filling is used up.

Place each kiss on a lightly greased, or parchment paper–lined, cookie sheet. Bake for 10–12 minutes, or until golden and crispy. Place on a platter; sprinkle with additional chopped chives and serve immediately.

Everything You Need to Know about Phyllo

Phyllo is a type of pastry most of us could not imagine making from scratch, but luckily it is widely available in most food stores. Some brands are better than others, but I have found the trick is to handle it with grace and care. Here are some simple guidelines for working with phyllo that will help you not to be intimidated by it.

1. *If the phyllo is frozen, thaw it completely before unfolding. This will take about 2 hours at room temperature.*
2. *Cover the unfolded sheets with a slightly damp tea towel to keep the pastry from drying out.*
3. *Have a clean, smooth, dry surface with enough space to work on.*
4. *Use a soft, clean brush for brushing the butter on.*
5. *Don't overbutter, as the phyllo will become soggy.*
6. *When filling smaller pieces of phyllo, place the filling on several pieces, and then fold or wrap them all, rather than wrapping each piece as you fill it.*
7. *Have your cookie sheet ready and the oven preheated.*
8. *You can make filled phyllo items ahead and then freeze them uncooked. To cook, thaw them at room temperature on a cookie sheet, and place them in the preheated oven until golden brown and crispy. The baking time will depend on the size of the pieces.*
9. *Line the cookie sheet with parchment paper, as it prevents the phyllo from becoming soggy on the bottom.*
10. *Don't use too much filling.*

Lemon Oregano Roast Leg of Lamb

The Greek method for basting lamb is the secret to its tenderness.

Serves 6 or more

  5 cloves garlic, finely chopped
  Juice of 2 lemons
  ½ cup (120 mL) fresh Greek oregano
  2 Tbsp. (30 mL) fresh lemon thyme leaves
  1 cup (240 mL) extra virgin olive oil
  Salt and freshly ground black pepper, to taste
  5- to 8-lb. (2.25- to 3.6-kg) leg of lamb
  3 cloves garlic, thinly sliced
  1 cup (240 mL) vegetable, meat or chicken stock
  3–4 bay leaves

Preheat the oven to 400°F (200°C).

Combine the finely chopped garlic, lemon juice, oregano, thyme and olive oil to make a marinade. Season with salt and pepper.

Trim the excess fat from the lamb. Slit the lamb in several places and insert the thinly sliced garlic. Put the stock and bay leaves in the roasting pan and place the lamb into the pan. Brush the lamb with the marinade.

Roast for 1–1 ½ hours, basting generously with the marinade every 15 minutes. Turn the oven down to 350°F (175°C) after the second basting (½ hour). Check with a meat thermometer for preferred doneness.

Remove the lamb from the oven and let it rest for 10–15 minutes before serving. Cut some slices off the leg, and arrange them beside the whole leg on a platter decorated with sprigs of oregano and lemon slices.

Briam—Mixed Roasted Vegetables

Traditional Greek recipes for briam are drenched in olive oil. I used half the amount and incorporated more fresh herbs.

Serves 6 or more

> 1 medium eggplant
> 2 medium zucchinis
> 3 potatoes
> 2 green or yellow sweet peppers
> 2 carrots
> 2 medium onions
> 1 14-oz. (398-mL) can crushed tomatoes or 3–4 fresh tomatoes, lightly blanched, peeled and chopped
> 1 cup (240 mL) water
> ½ cup (120 mL) olive oil
> 2 cloves garlic, finely chopped
> 1 cup (240 mL) mixed fresh tarragon, parsley, chives and rosemary
> Salt and freshly ground black pepper, to taste

Preheat the oven to 350°F (175°C).

Cut all the fresh vegetables into quarters. Combine all the ingredients in a casserole, reserving ½ cup (120 mL) of the mixed herbs. Bake for 45 minutes, or until tender. Sprinkle with the reserved herbs and serve immediately.

Ouzo Orange Ice

A unique licorice-flavored palate cleanser.

Serves 6

>   3 cups (720 mL) freshly squeezed orange juice
>   1 cup (240 mL) ouzo
>   Juice of 1 lemon
>   1 cup (240 mL) granulated sugar
>   1 tsp. (5 mL) finely chopped tarragon
>   2 oranges, peeled and broken into segments
>   6 small sprigs fresh tarragon

Combine the orange juice, ouzo, lemon juice and sugar in a heavy saucepan over medium heat. Stir constantly until the mixture is about to boil and all the sugar is dissolved.

Cool to room temperature. Add the tarragon. Pour into a shallow container such as an 8-inch (20-cm) cake tin, or place in an ice cream maker and prepare according to manufacturer's instructions. Let the mixture freeze overnight, or for a few hours. Break the ice up in a food processor and return it to the freezer until it's firm, but soft enough to scoop. Serve in wine glasses and garnish each glass with a few orange segments and a sprig of tarragon.

Tarragon Spring Lunch

This salute to tarragon celebrates spring rebirth and the arrival of this aromatic herb in the garden. The flavor of tarragon is woven throughout all the recipes. You may choose to use one or two of the dishes in combination with other menus.

Tarragon White Bean Dip

*Roasted Organic Tarragon Chicken
with Chardonnay Tarragon Sauce*

Citrus Spring Vegetable Orzo with Tarragon and Chives

*Grilled Endive and Onion Salad
with Thyme Tarragon Vinaigrette*

Rhubarb Tart with Sweet Cicely and Toasted Almond Cream

Tarragon

This herb has a reputation for losing its flavor after growing for four years in the same place. Not in our experience. We find that if the plants are top-dressed with compost as they break out of their winter dormancy in February, the flavor is maintained for at least eight years.

Tarragon is a native of Russia and is reliably hardy here, but it doesn't like wet feet. Flatland gardeners might try it in a raised bed. Container growing is fine for one year, but the roots will soon fill anything smaller than a half-barrel.

Tarragon White Bean Dip

A quick, delicious appetizer. Serve it with breadsticks or interesting crackers.

Makes approximately 2 cups (475 mL)

> 2 cloves garlic
> Salt and freshly ground black pepper, to taste
> 2 Tbsp. (30 mL) fresh tarragon
> 2 Tbsp. (30 mL) lemon juice
> 2 cups (475 mL) cooked white cannellini beans
> ½ cup (120 mL) extra virgin olive oil

In a food processor, blend the garlic, salt and pepper. Add the tarragon and blend again. Add the lemon juice and beans, and blend until smooth.

Taste for seasoning. While the motor is running, slowly add the olive oil. Place in a serving bowl and decorate with a sprig of tarragon.

Roasted Organic Tarragon Chicken
with Chardonnay Tarragon Sauce

Celebrate the assertive taste of tarragon with this organic chicken.

Serves 6–8

> 1 whole 5- to 6-lb. (2.25- to 2.8-kg) free-range roasting chicken
> ⅓ cup (80 mL) virgin olive oil
> Juice of 1 lemon
> 1 onion, cut into quarters
> 1 large bunch tarragon
> 3 cloves garlic, sliced
> 1 recipe Chardonnay Tarragon Sauce (see page 50)

Preheat the oven to 400°F (200°C).

Rinse and pat the chicken dry, and place it in an ovenproof pan. Rub the chicken with olive oil, massaging it in gently. Squeeze the lemon juice over the chicken. Stuff the squeezed lemon halves, onion quarters, and a handful of tarragon inside the chicken's cavity. Loosen the breast skin and slide the sliced garlic and some more tarragon under the skin. Roast the chicken for approximately 1½ hours. It is done when the juice runs clear, and the legs move easily.

Let the chicken rest for 15 minutes. To serve, place it on a bed of tarragon on a platter and decorate with tarragon sprigs. Pass the Chardonnay Tarragon Sauce separately.

Chardonnay Tarragon Sauce

Makes 1½–2 cups (360–475 mL)

2 large shallots, peeled and finely chopped

3 cloves garlic, finely chopped

1 cup (240 mL) dry, fruity white wine, such as Chardonnay

2 cups (475 mL) chicken stock

1 tsp. (5 mL) lemon zest

1 Tbsp. (15 mL) Dijon mustard

1 Tbsp. (15 mL) finely chopped tarragon

Juice of 1 lemon

½ cup (60 mL) heavy cream (optional)

Salt and freshly ground black pepper, to taste

Remove any excess fat and tarragon from the roasting pan. Place the pan over medium heat and sauté the shallots and garlic for 1–2 minutes.

Deglaze the pan with the wine, simmering until the liquid is reduced by half. Add the chicken stock and lemon zest and reduce again by approximately a third. Whisk in the mustard and finely chopped tarragon, lemon juice and cream. Bring back to a gentle simmer and taste for seasoning. Serve on the side with the chicken.

Citrus Spring Vegetable Orzo with Tarragon and Chives

Orzo absorbs the flavors of tarragon and citrus beautifully.

Serves 6

½ cup (120 mL) extra virgin olive oil
1 red onion, finely chopped
2 cloves garlic, finely chopped
1 sweet red pepper, finely chopped
1 sweet yellow pepper, finely chopped
1 medium zucchini, finely chopped
1 Tbsp. (15 mL) lemon zest
1 Tbsp. (15 mL) orange zest
1 lb. (455 g) orzo, cooked al dente (5–6 minutes), rinsed and set aside
Salt and freshly ground black pepper, to taste
½ cup (120 mL) finely chopped fresh tarragon
½ cup (120 mL) finely chopped fresh chives
Juice of 1 orange
Juice of 1 lemon
2 Tbsp. (30 mL) white wine vinegar
½ cup (120 mL) freshly grated Parmesan cheese
Sprigs fresh tarragon

Heat a large frying pan over medium heat and add 2 Tbsp. (30 mL) of the olive oil. Add the onion and garlic and sweat them for 2–3 minutes. Add the peppers, zucchini and lemon and orange zest, and sauté for another 2 minutes.

Put the orzo in a large serving bowl. Toss with the rest of the olive oil, salt, pepper, tarragon, chives, sautéed vegetables, orange and lemon juice, and white wine vinegar. Sprinkle with the Parmesan cheese and garnish with tarragon sprigs.

Endive

*One way of growing the
Belgian or Witloof endive
is to sow the seeds in May
or early June in rich soil
and water every three or
four days, if the weather is
dry. In early November, the
leaves should be cut off
about 1 inch (2.5 cm) above
the top of the root. The
roots are then covered
with 6 inches (15 cm)
of sawdust. The tender
endive chicons are ready
for harvesting in late
February and March.*

*A second way, which
produces the tender tops in
December, January and
February, is to dig up the
white carrotlike tap root.
Cut off the leaves and bury
the roots close together in
peat moss in a plastic pail.
The roots should then be
stored in a cool, dark place.
Move them to a warm,
dark place for three weeks
before you want to eat the
tender edibles.*

Grilled Endive and Onion Salad with Thyme Tarragon Vinaigrette

The slightly tart taste of the endive goes well with the sweet onion. For a pretty presentation, decorate with thyme and chive flowers.

Serves 4–6

> 2 Tbsp. (30 mL) thyme, finely chopped
> 3 Tbsp. (45 mL) fresh tarragon, finely chopped
> 2 Tbsp. (30 mL) red wine vinegar
> 1 Tbsp. (15 mL) Dijon mustard
> Salt and freshly ground black pepper, to taste
> ½ cup (120 mL) extra virgin olive oil
> 4 bunches fresh Belgian endive, washed, dried and halved lengthwise
> 2 red onions, sliced ⅛ inch (.3 cm) thick

Preheat the barbecue to medium.

Whisk the thyme, tarragon, vinegar, mustard, salt and pepper in a small bowl. While continuing to whisk, slowly add the olive oil in a steady stream until emulsified. Check for seasoning.

Brush the endive and onion lightly with vinaigrette. Grill for approximately 2 minutes per side, or until slightly soft. Arrange on a small platter and drizzle with the remaining vinaigrette.

Rhubarb Tart with Sweet Cicely and Toasted Almond Cream

The first fruit-of-the-season dessert from the garden.

Serves 8

For the pastry:

2½ cups (600 mL) unbleached all purpose flour
1 tsp. (5 mL) salt
4 tsp. (20 mL) granulated sugar
½ lb. (225 g) cold butter, cut in pieces
1 egg, beaten
3–4 Tbsp. (45–60 mL) ice water

Preheat the oven to 375°F (190°C).

Combine the flour, salt and sugar in a mixing bowl. Working quickly, cut in the butter with your fingertips or a pastry cutter, until the mixture resembles coarse bread crumbs. Combine the egg and ice water. Sprinkle the liquid, 1–2 Tbsp. (15–30 mL) at a time over the flour mixture. When you can gather the dough into a ball, you've added enough water. Knead gently and briefly to blend the butter and smooth the dough. Flatten the dough slightly, wrap it in plastic wrap or waxed paper, and refrigerate for 30 minutes.

Roll the chilled dough out on a lightly floured surface to approximately ¼ inch (.6 cm) thickness. Transfer to a 12-inch (30-cm) tart pan and press it into the bottom and sides of the pan. Trim the dough, leaving a 1-inch (2.5-cm) overhang. Fold the overhang back toward the inside, and crimp the edge decoratively.

Prick the bottom with a fork. Line the pastry with aluminum foil or parchment, and fill the pan with pie weights or dried beans. Bake the pastry for 8–10 minutes. Remove the foil and weights and return the pastry to the oven. Bake until golden brown, 10–13 minutes more. Set aside to cool.

For the almond cream:
   ¾ cup (180 mL) soft butter
   1½ cups (360 mL) ground almonds, toasted
   ½ cup (120 mL) sugar
   2 eggs
   2 Tbsp. (30 mL) rum

Blend the butter, almonds and sugar. Add the eggs one at a time. Mix in the rum. Blend well, cover and refrigerate if you will not be baking the tart within 15 minutes.

For the rhubarb:
   5–6 cups (1.2–1.5 L) finely chopped rhubarb
   2 Tbsp. (30 mL) tapioca
   3 Tbsp. (45 mL) finely chopped sweet cicely
   1 cup (240 mL) sugar
   Juice and zest of 1 orange
   ½ cup (120 mL) water

Combine the rhubarb, tapioca, sweet cicely, sugar, orange juice and zest, and water in a medium saucepan. Simmer gently for 5–10 minutes, or until the rhubarb is tender.

To assemble:
   2 Tbsp. (30 mL) melted jelly of your choice
   3–4 small sprigs sweet cicely
   Icing sugar

Preheat the oven to 325°F (165°C).

Spoon the almond cream into the tart shell. Arrange the rhubarb on top. Bake for 20 minutes. Remove from the oven and place on a rack to cool. Brush the rhubarb lightly with your favorite jelly. Decorate with sweet cicely sprigs and a light sprinkling of icing sugar.

Spirited Sunday Brunch

Sunday Brunch is a very relaxing way to entertain friends. Kids and dogs can mill around. The Bullshot Lovage Soup will relax the adults, and the big garlic tortilla will fill everyone up. Take a Sunday walk, have a light supper and an early night.

Bullshot Lovage-Infused Soup

Ravenhill Buttermilk Scones

Potato Garlic Tortilla with Sorrel and Chives

Pork and Dried Cranberry Sage Patties with
Caramelized Apples

Bullshot Lovage-Infused Soup

A perfect hair-of-the-dog remedy with the option of adding vodka.

Serves 4–6

> 1 Tbsp. (15 mL) olive oil
>
> 2 celery stalks, finely chopped
>
> 1 carrot, finely chopped
>
> 1 shallot, finely chopped
>
> 2 cloves garlic, finely chopped
>
> 2 sprigs lovage, coarsely chopped
>
> Salt and freshly ground black pepper, to taste
>
> 6 Tbsp. (90 mL) good-quality vodka (optional)
>
> 4 cups (950 mL) tomato juice
>
> 2 cups (475 mL) chicken or vegetable stock
>
> Hot pepper sauce, to taste
>
> Worcestershire sauce, to taste
>
> 4–6 whole lovage leaves
>
> 1 lemon, sliced

Heat a soup or casserole pot over medium heat. Add the olive oil, celery, carrot, shallot, garlic, lovage, salt and pepper. Sauté for 2 minutes. Deglaze with 2 Tbsp. (30 mL) vodka, simmering for 1 minute. Add the tomato juice and stock, and simmer gently for 15 minutes.

While the soup is simmering, set out 4–6 soup bowls or large mugs. Put 1 Tbsp. (15 mL) vodka in each, add a dash of hot pepper sauce and a dash of Worcestershire sauce. Strain the soup. Pour into the bowls. Decorate each with a leaf of lovage and a slice of lemon.

Ravenhill Buttermilk Scones

I adapted this recipe from Fernhill Lodge on Mayne Island. It is well tested and most delicious.

Serves 6–8

> 2 cups (475 mL) all purpose flour
>
> 4 tsp. (20 mL) baking powder
>
> ½ tsp. (2.5 mL) salt
>
> 2 Tbsp. (30 mL) sugar
>
> 6 Tbsp. (90 mL) butter
>
> ½ cup (120 mL) buttermilk
>
> 2 eggs
>
> ½ cup (120 mL) currants, cranberries or other berries (optional)

Preheat the oven to 425°F (220°C).

Sift the flour, baking powder, salt and sugar. Add the butter to the sifted ingredients and blend until the mixture resembles a fine meal. Beat the buttermilk with the eggs until light. Reserve 2 tsp. (10 mL) and add the remainder to the dry ingredients, stirring only until the flour is dampened. Add the fruit, if desired.

Knead the dough 20 times and roll it out into a circle ¾ inch (2 cm) thick. Place on a lightly greased cookie sheet. Brush with the reserved milk/egg mixture. Cut into pie-shaped pieces. Bake for 10–12 minutes. Serve warm with your favorite jams.

Potato Garlic Tortilla with Sorrel and Chives

My Spanish friend used to make this tortilla for picnics. I've added more herbs—because that's what we do! The balsamic glaze is delicious brushed on any dish that suits a tangy, savory glaze.

Serves 8

> 3 medium potatoes
> ¼ cup (60 mL) extra virgin olive oil
> 5 cloves garlic, finely chopped
> 4 eggs, beaten in a large bowl
> 1 cup (240 mL) mixed sorrel and chives, finely chopped
> Salt and freshly ground black pepper, to taste
> ½ cup (120 mL) balsamic vinegar
> Chive blossoms

Blanch the potatoes until they are easily sliced, but not completely cooked. Slice them approximately ¼ inch (.6 cm) thick.

Heat the olive oil over medium heat in a large, well-seasoned or non-stick frying pan. Add the potato, and sauté for approximately 10 minutes, until lightly browned. Toss the garlic with the potatoes.

Beat the eggs in a large bowl and add the potatoes. Add the sorrel and chives and season with salt and pepper.

Transfer the mixture back into the frying pan, and cook over medium-low heat until solid, but slightly wet on top. Place under the broiler for 1 minute or until the top begins to brown. Flip the tortilla over onto a large plate.

Place the balsamic vinegar in a small saucepan. Cook until it's reduced by half, or until it has a syrupy consistency.

To serve, brush the tortilla with the balsamic glaze and sprinkle with chive flowers.

Pork and Dried Cranberry Sage Patties with Caramelized Apples

Bored with plain old pork chops and applesauce? This is a slightly more sophisticated dish than the old standby.

Serves 4–6

> 1 lb. (455 g) lean ground pork
> ½ cup (120 mL) dried cranberries, rehydrated in hot water for
>   5 minutes and drained
> 3 Tbsp. (45 mL) finely chopped fresh young sage
> 2 shallots, finely chopped
> Salt and freshly ground pepper to taste
> ½ cup (120 mL) flour
> 2 Tbsp. (30 mL) olive oil

Combine the pork, cranberries, sage, shallots and salt and pepper. Mix well and form into 8–10 patties. Lightly dust the patties with flour. Heat the oil in a large frying pan over medium heat. Cook the patties for approximately 4 minutes per side. Serve with Caramelized Apples.

Caramelized Apples

> 6–7 medium-size tart apples, peeled and cored
> 2 Tbsp. (30 mL) unsalted butter
> ⅔ cup (160 mL) granulated sugar
> 2 Tbsp. (30 mL) fresh mint, finely chopped

Cut the apples into thin slices. Melt the butter over medium heat in a large heavy frying pan. Add the sugar and gently cook until the sugar becomes a light, golden brown. Add the apple slices, mix well, and reduce the heat to low. Cover and cook for 15 minutes. Remove the cover, raise the heat to medium, and cook until the pan juices are syrupy. Sprinkle with fresh mint.

May
and
June

Vegetable Indulgences:
Asparagus and Artichokes

Artichoke—the vegetable of which one has more at the finish than at the start of the dinner.

—Lord Chesterfield

Eating an artichoke is like eating a goddamned pine cone.

—My brother-in-law

The artichoke is a trick vegetable.

—Groucho Marx

Eating an artichoke is like getting to know someone really well.

—Willi Hastings

MAY AND JUNE are less tentative months in the garden. There are more vegetables to harvest and eat. For me, the two leading lights of the vegetable garden at this time are asparagus and artichokes. I can have dinners that consist of one large white plate filled with either a stack of asparagus or three to four artichokes—and, of course, some melted butter and a large glass of white wine.

I first encountered fresh artichokes—acres and acres of spiky blue architectural plants—while driving on the coast south of San Francisco in the sixties. It was a wondrous sight for someone who had only eaten canned artichoke hearts. We stopped at a stand and bought a bagful, and cooked them for supper with some lemon butter. I became a confirmed artichoke devotee. Back home, when we were haunting nurseries for plants for the garden, I was thrilled to find some artichoke plants. I did not know if they would grow in a B.C. coastal garden but I quickly took them back to the farm, and Andrew planted them with lots of rich compost. They have been in the garden ever since and have been divided and moved several times.

When we first came to the farm there was an asparagus bed, a wonderful gift left by a former owner. We have been eating asparagus from it now for 20 years, and for a brief five weeks it is the favorite vegetable of which one never tires. Alice B. Toklas felt asparagus should be no thicker than a darning needle when picked. Too thin for me. I like it chunky, not wispy. When the asparagus first comes up in the spring, I wander by the patch and surreptitiously snap off a couple of spears to munch, but not before checking to make sure that Andrew the gardener is not watching, for he guards his future dinners carefully. The asparagus tastes of raw spring energy, and I am sure it is a tonic for the body and the digestive system. I have heard tales of wild asparagus growing in ditches in the Okanagan from a friend who was a botanical collector for the government. She snacked along the ditches while doing her research. Which reminds me of a subtle, simple quote by Curnonsky, a famous chef and cookbook writer, "Cuisine is when things taste like themselves."

There are two asparagus farms in our area. One grows the type of fat white asparagus they have in Europe, and one near our farm grows regular green asparagus. I am a firm believer in saving agricultural land from development and I think asparagus farms should be encouraged and subsidized just as other crops in Canada are. I can visualize fields of asparagus fronds waving all over the peninsula, and city folk driving out to the country on asparagus pilgrimages, and farmers organizing asparagus festivals with huge pots of melted butter. But my fantasies are running away with me.

In the very center of our garden is a large dogwood tree that blooms in May. It looks like a giant bride dressed in a gown of creamy white flowers. By late spring the barn swallows return, and they hustle about checking their old nests. Most of them are near a light bulb, which probably gives the birds extra warmth. The violet-green swallows nest in boxes outside the barn, and often quarrel with the house sparrows over a little shake-roofed birdhouse I can watch from the kitchen window. Some years the sparrows win and sometimes the swallows move in. The roses are putting on a show and they flourish if I can inveigle enough compost for them. There seems to be an unspoken compost rule that vegetables get it first. A very pragmatic rule, but there should be room for both food and beauty, and compost for all.

Besides wild hatches of baby birds there are hatches of domestic fowl. Sometimes their nests are precarious. The two white female geese make nests behind an old, once-white bathtub. They pluck down from their heaving bosoms and add it to the straw, grass and twigs they use to line their nests. These two sister geese lay quantities of eggs, which get all in a muddle. Some eggs roll out of the nests onto the grass. They sit on each other's eggs, and if you come near and peer over the stone wall they hiss and scream at you. We always intend to write down the day they start sitting, but somehow the thought never gets translated to the day book. Thirty days can pass and nothing happens. This year, one goose gave up, but her sister goose remained sitting, and, lo and behold, she produced four downy, vivid, yellow fluffballs. Immediately the three other geese—one female and two males—moved in as parents. Despite all this communal parenting, two goslings were done in by marauding ravens. One had its chest pierced; we nursed it one night in a box, but it did not survive. The other gosling disappeared in the meadow without a trace or a yellow fluffy feather to be found. The remaining two goslings stayed close to their communal parents and survived the raven attacks. They are now young, rowdy teenagers and are free of any imminent danger. Three peacocks produced one brown pheasant-like chick with an amazing punk topknot. Its life was brief also, as it drowned in a bucket of water. Life in the barnyard can have all the tragedy and drama of an opera. There is lust, fear, tragic death, and lots of noisy fowl music chorusing in the back-ground.

Meanwhile, back in the garden, fava beans, also known as broad beans, are happening. These fat juicy beans in their fuzzy lined pod cases are beloved by Italians and the English. They are delicate when tiny, and can be eaten raw with coarse French salt as a nibble before dinner. This was my English father's favorite vegetable, though it seems we usually ate them when they were larger, tougher and boiled to death. When the beans are older the outer skins can be very tough and nasty to chew, but if you simmer them and remove this rugged carapace, the inner bean is soft and delicious and a superb vegetable. An Italian friend said his family deep-fried the green tops of fava beans. Andrew cooks the young beans with chopped mint, and some garlic and a little olive oil. This is quite a sprightly dish served with a lamb chop and a new potato.

Other May/June edible treasures are green peas, new arugula and lettuce. We have found a red lettuce that seeds itself and there are little red lettuce planta-tions sprinkled all over the garden. And then, of course, there are strawberries in June. We live in strawberry country, so if ours are late, or not very productive, we can slowly drive down Oldfield Road and find some. Mostly we eat them for breakfast. This is the one fruit that makes those healthy bran cereals acceptable. It takes away the dubious puritan pleasure of eating a high-fiber cereal. Others like the strawberries too. The dogs snuffle them through the net. Birds come and steal them, and marauding

Fava Beans

The varieties 'Aquadulce' and 'Broad Windsor' can both be sown in late October or early November for harvesting in May. Spring-sown broad beans are more likely to be infested with black aphids. If the aphids do get established, even picking off the tender top growth only slows them down. On the plus side, aphids provide food for ladybugs.

nephews and nieces have been known to return to the house with a telltale red stain ringing their rosy lips. Andrew makes his old-fashioned jam without liquid fruit pectin. It has to be watched like a hawk or it turns to red cement.

The menus chosen for this season contain all the fruit and vegetables mentioned here. There is an artichoke celebration, a summer wedding lunch with homemade strawberry ice cream, and an asparagus lover's dinner.

May and June can be very mixed months weather-wise. One evening you are eating your artichokes on the patio, watching the swallows swoop over the pool, getting their last drink before dark, and the next evening it is gray and rainy and you want to light the fire. The rain is good for peas and lettuce and other salad greens, but by the end of June I am whining for heat, and wishing for tomatoes and basil. I must be patient, for the garden will provide.

Seductive Artichokes
and Artful Asparagus

May and June bring wonderful things from the garden, farms and markets, but asparagus and artichokes are some of the most seductive. We look forward all year to the brief season when they are at their peak.

Steamed Artichokes with a Chervil Chive Butter

Tomato Bruschetta with Olives, Arugula and Parmesan

Saltimbocca Pappardelle with Fresh Asparagus

Lemon Lemon Balm Sorbet

Steamed Artichokes with a Chervil Chive Butter

Eating a whole artichoke is a social, sensuous experience. The hidden heart is the pièce de résistance.

Serves 4

> 4 fresh whole artichokes
> ½ cup (120 mL) butter
> Juice of 1 lemon
> ¼ cup (60 mL) fresh chervil leaves
> ¼ cup (60 mL) finely chopped fresh chives
> Salt and freshly ground black pepper, to taste

Rinse the artichokes under cold water, spreading the leaves apart to wash off any grit. Slice off the top 1 inch (2.5 cm) of the cone. Cut off the top ½ inch (1.2 cm) of each of the remaining leaves with scissors. Rub all cut portions with lemon. Cut off the end of the stem if it is woody. Pull off any small leaves around the bottom, rubbing it again with lemon.

Arrange the artichokes upside-down in one layer in a steaming basket placed inside a large pot. Pour at least 1 to 2 inches (2.5 to 5 cm) of water into the pot. Simmer covered for 30–40 minutes, periodically checking the water level. The artichokes are done when the bottoms are tender when pierced with a small knife and the leaves pull off easily. The inside flesh on the leaf should be tender when scraped off between your teeth.

While the artichokes are cooking, make the chervil chive butter. Combine the butter, lemon juice, chervil and chives in a small pot over low heat. Do not boil. Keep the mixture warm until serving time.

Present each person with an artichoke and a side dish of butter. Place a larger bowl in the center of the table for the discarded leaves. Start with the leaves at the bottom of the artichoke. Remove one and, holding it by the top, dip the large bottom end into the butter and then scrape the tender flesh between your teeth.

When you come to the tender cone of central leaves, pull off the cone, and eat the bottom portion. In the spot where the cone was removed is a cluster of small leaves. Beneath these leaves is a hairy growth (the choke), which covers the deliciously edible bottom heart of the artichoke. Gently scrape out and discard the hairy portion. Cut the bottom into wedges, dip them into the butter, and ascend to heaven.

Tomato Bruschetta with Olives, Arugula and Parmesan

If possible, try to use baby arugula in this dish. You can substitute watercress for the arugula.

Makes 20 pieces

> 6 medium tomatoes, coarsely chopped into small pieces
> ½ cup (120 mL) pitted and finely chopped Moroccan olives
> 3 cloves garlic, finely chopped or pressed
> 2 tsp. (10 mL) balsamic vinegar
> ½ cup (120 mL) finely chopped fresh chives
> Salt and freshly ground black pepper, to taste
> 1 long baguette or 2 short baguettes
> ¼ cup (60 mL) extra virgin olive oil
> 1 cup (240 mL) arugula leaves
> 1 cup (240 mL) shaved or slivered Parmesan cheese

Combine the tomatoes, olives, garlic, vinegar, chives and salt and pepper in a bowl. If the tomatoes are watery, drain them before combining with the other ingredients.

Cut the baguette into slices approximately ¼ inch (.6 cm) thick. Lightly toast, if desired, and brush lightly with olive oil. Place the arugula on the bread and spoon the tomato mixture on top. Place some cheese on top. Serve as is, or place under the broiler for 1 minute to melt the cheese.

Saltimbocca Pappardelle with Fresh Asparagus

Saltimbocca literally means "jump in your mouth." There is a classic veal dish by this name, but here I'm simply using the predominant flavors of prosciutto and sage with my favorite pasta to create an intensely delicious and nourishing broth.

Serves 4

> 1 lb. (455 g) asparagus, washed and trimmed of woody ends
> 3 Tbsp. (45 mL) olive oil
> 6 cloves garlic, finely chopped
> 3 shallots, finely chopped
> 8 oz. (225 g) prosciutto, finely chopped
> 2 Tbsp. (30 mL) finely chopped fresh sage
> 1 cup (240 mL) dry white wine or dry white vermouth
> 4 cups (950 mL) hot chicken or vegetable stock
> ½ cup (120 mL) heavy cream (optional)
> 1 lb. (455 g) pappardelle pasta
> 8 oz. (225 g) freshly grated Parmesan cheese
> 4 sprigs sage

In a large pot of simmering salted water, blanch the asparagus for 2–3 minutes, until tender. Remove and plunge into cold water. When it is cool, drain and set aside. Reserve the cooking water for the pasta.

Heat a large heavy casserole over medium heat. Add the olive oil, garlic, shallots, prosciutto and sage. Sauté for 2–3 minutes. Add the wine and simmer for 1 minute. Add the stock and simmer for approximately 10 minutes. Turn the heat to low. Taste for seasoning. Add the cream, if desired, whisking it in slowly.

While the broth is simmering, bring the asparagus water back to a boil and cook the pasta for 8–10 minutes, until al dente. Drain the pasta and divide among 4 bowls. Place the asparagus in the broth to warm it, and then ladle the broth and asparagus into each bowl. Sprinkle with fresh Parmesan and garnish with a fresh sage sprig.

Lemon Lemon Balm Sorbet

A refreshing sorbet to clean and stimulate the palate. If desired, pour a dash of sparkling wine on top.

Serves 4

> 1 cup (240 mL) lemon juice, chilled
> ¼ cup (60 mL) finely chopped lemon balm leaves
> 1 cup (240 mL) sugar syrup (see sidebar)
> 1 tsp. (5 mL) lemon zest, finely chopped

Combine all the ingredients. Place in a chilled ice cream maker and follow the manufacturer's instructions, or pour into a thin metal bowl and freeze for 2 hours. Remove the sorbet, break it up by hand or in a food processor, and place it back in the freezer until it has a firm consistency.

Serve in flutes or wine glasses.

Sugar Syrup

To make a simple sugar syrup, place 2 cups (475 mL) water and 2 cups (475 mL) sugar in a saucepan. Bring to a simmer and stir until the sugar is dissolved. Cool to room temperature. Refrigerate in a sealed jar. This syrup will keep up to a month. Make sure it is very cold before using it in a sorbet.

Summer Wedding Lunch

This elegant lunch was inspired by my wedding dinner, held in the garden at Ravenhill.

Wild Rice Crêpes with Creamed Garlic Mushrooms

*Butter Lettuce Salad with Roasted Almonds and
Nasturtium Chervil Chive Vinaigrette*

Barbecued Wild Coho Salmon with Salal Berry Chutney

Fresh Herb Risotto

Homemade Strawberry Ice Cream

Mint Madeleines

Wild Rice Crêpes with Creamed Garlic Mushrooms

This was my wedding hors d'oeuvre, made with chanterelles. Add interest by using mushrooms other than white button mushrooms.

Makes 12 crêpes

For the crêpes:

    1 cup (240 mL) unbleached all purpose flour
    1 Tbsp. (15 mL) sugar
    ¼ tsp. (1.2 mL) salt
    1 cup (240 mL) milk
    ⅓ cup (80 mL) water
    3 eggs
    3 Tbsp. (45 mL) unsalted butter, melted
    ½ cup (120 mL) cooked wild rice
    2 Tbsp. (30 mL) finely chopped fresh tarragon

Combine the flour, sugar and salt in a food processor and process briefly. With the motor running, slowly add the milk, water, eggs and butter, one at a time. Process until smooth. Add the wild rice and tarragon, and process briefly.

Heat a 7 inch (18 cm) non-stick frying pan (or a well-seasoned carbon steel crêpe pan) over medium heat until the pan is quite hot. Pour in 3 Tbsp. (45 mL) of batter and quickly tilt the pan so the batter spreads evenly in a thin layer over the bottom of the pan. Cook 30–40 seconds, then turn and cook another 15–20 seconds.

Repeat with the remaining batter, stacking the crêpes with a layer of parchment or wax paper between each crêpe. Wrap securely in plastic wrap and refrigerate if you will not be serving the crêpes immediately.

Garlic

The mature garlic harvest starts in July, but the planting takes place in October. Garlic needs a rich, weed-free soil and good supplies of nitrogen in late February and the middle of March. Store the harvested bulbs at house temperature in a dry place, rather than in a cool, moist area. We grow four types.

- *Elephant garlic, for soups and stocks.*
- *Rocambole, a sweet and crisply tender variety, has the curious habit of making a loop in its flower spike. It is superb baked with a little olive oil and balsamic vinegar. Rocambole doesn't keep well much beyond November.*
- *'French Red' is our main early crop.*
- *'Chinese White' is the long-keeping variety. It forms a small bulb that lasts until harvesting begins again.*

For the mushroom filling:

1 Tbsp. (15 mL) butter
2 shallots, finely chopped
3 cloves garlic, finely chopped
1 tsp. (5 mL) flour
1 lb. (455 g) mushrooms, preferably brown or
    wild or a mixture of the two, sliced
¼ cup (60 mL) fortified wine, such as Marsala,
    Madeira, port or sherry
1 cup (240 mL) whipping cream
1 Tbsp. (15 mL) fresh thyme leaves
Salt and freshly ground black pepper, to taste
1 Tbsp. (15 mL) finely chopped fresh chives

Melt the butter in a large frying pan over medium-low heat. Add the shallots and garlic and cook for 5 minutes. Sprinkle with flour and stir to combine. Add the mushrooms and sauté for 2–3 minutes. Add the wine and simmer for 1 minute. Stir in the cream and thyme. Simmer over low heat until the mixture has thickened slightly, approximately 5–10 minutes. Season with salt and pepper and add the chives.

To assemble:

Spoon about 2 Tbsp. (30 mL) of warm creamed mushrooms onto each crêpe. Fold the crêpe into quarters. Layer the folded crêpes on a platter. Garnish with a few more chives and some edible flowers.

Butter Lettuce with Roasted Almonds and Nasturtium Chervil Chive Vinaigrette

Andrew grows beautiful, crunchy little "Tom Thumb" butter lettuces, but any fresh lettuce centers will do for this recipe.

Serves 4

> 4 small butter lettuce heads or 2–3 large butter lettuce or romaine
>   heads, split in half and the large outer leaves removed
> ½ cup (120 mL) whole almonds
> ½ tsp. (2.5 mL) salt
> 1 tsp. (5 mL) sugar
> ¼ cup (60 mL) lemon juice
> ¼ cup (60 mL) finely chopped chives or green onion
> 2 Tbsp. (30 mL) finely chopped nasturtium flowers
> 1 Tbsp. (15 mL) chervil leaves
> 1 Tbsp. (15 mL) Dijon mustard
> ½ cup (120 mL) extra virgin olive oil
> Salt and freshly ground pepper, to taste

Wash and dry the lettuce. Spread the almonds on a cookie sheet and dry roast in a preheated 325°F (165°C) oven for approximately 10–15 minutes. Remove from the oven and toss with salt and sugar. Set aside.

In a bowl, combine the lemon juice, chives or onion, nasturtium flowers, chervil and mustard. Whisk in the oil gradually, until the dressing is emulsified. Taste and season with salt and pepper.

Place a small, whole lettuce on each plate. Sprinkle with almonds. Drizzle with vinaigrette and decorate with more nasturtiums and chervil sprigs.

Barbecued Wild Coho Salmon with Salal Berry Chutney

In the summer, Andrew and Noël drive to the fish market on the Sidney wharf and buy just-caught wild Coho salmon. Their long-awaited basil crop is flourishing, so they use it in the salmon marinade. Noël and I created this recipe together. You can use all sweet basil or a combination, such as lemon, opal and lettuce leaf basils.

Serves 8

> 1 4- to 6-lb. (1.8- to 2.7-kg) salmon, tail and head removed,
>   filleted and butterflied
> 1 cup (240 mL) basil
> ½ cup (120 mL) white wine
> ¼ cup (60 mL) rice wine vinegar
> 4 cloves garlic, finely chopped
> 2 shallots, peeled and finely chopped
> ¼ cup (60 mL) extra virgin olive oil
> ¼ cup (60 mL) soy sauce
> 2 tsp. (10 mL) sugar
> ½ tsp. (2.5 mL) sambal oelek (hot chili paste)
> ⅓ cup (80 mL) white wine
> ½ tsp. (2.5 mL) sugar
> Sprigs fresh basil
> 1 recipe Salal Berry Chutney (page 77)

Have the salmon ready. Combine the ingredients except for the ⅓ cup (75 mL) white wine, ½ tsp. (2.5 mL) sugar and basil sprigs. Reserve ¼ cup (60 mL) of the marinade for the sauce. Pour the remaining marinade over the salmon, coating it well. Place in the refrigerator for at least 1 hour, turning it every 15 minutes.

When the salmon has finished marinating, heat the reserved marinade, white wine and sugar in a small saucepan. Simmer gently for about 5 minutes. Keep warm over very low heat.

Meanwhile, lightly oil the barbecue and preheat it to medium-high. Place the salmon on the grill, flesh side down, at an angle. Rotate the salmon by 90 degrees after 2–3 minutes, so it will be marked in a diamond pattern by the grill. Grill for another 5 minutes. Flip over and grill for 2–3 minutes on the other side. The salmon should be slightly underdone as it will continue cooking once removed from the barbecue. The cooking time will vary, depending on the size of the fish and the heat of the barbecue. When done, it should be tender and will flake apart easily.

Place the salmon on a platter, pour the warm sauce over it and decorate with sprigs of basil. Serve with a bowl of Salal Berry Chutney.

Salal Berry Chutney

I adapted this recipe from Carrie Pollard, an excellent caterer who served this chutney with barbecued salmon at my wedding. The tart berries combine well with fish and game. Salal berries are mainly found wild in wooded areas and sometimes in established gardens. If you can't find fresh salal berries, try fresh cranberries or blueberries.

Makes approximately ¾ cup (180 mL)

> ½ cup (120 mL) sugar
> 3 Tbsp. (45 mL) water
> ¼ cup (60 mL) high-quality balsamic vinegar
> 1 cup (240 mL) crushed salal berries
> 1 medium red onion, thinly sliced
> 1 tsp. (5 mL) fresh thyme leaves
> 2 tsp. (10 mL) finely sliced ginger
> Salt and freshly ground black pepper, to taste

Combine the sugar and water in a saucepan over medium heat. Simmer until it turns a light golden color. Add the vinegar, berries, onion, thyme, ginger, salt and pepper. Simmer until the mixture is a syrupy consistency and is beautifully jeweled, approximately 10 minutes. Serve as a condiment with the salmon.

Fresh Herb Risotto

The lemon and lemon verbena spark up this herbed risotto. If you can't find lemon verbena, substitute 1 Tbsp. (15 mL) lemon zest and a bay leaf.

Serves 8

> 5–6 cups (1.2–1.5 L) chicken stock (use more if necessary)
> 4 lemon verbena leaves
> 2 Tbsp. (30 mL) butter
> 2 Tbsp. (30 mL) olive oil
> 3–4 shallots, peeled and chopped
> 2 cloves garlic, finely chopped
> 2 cups (475 mL) Arborio rice
> ½ cup (120 mL) freshly grated Parmesan cheese
> 1–2 cups (240–475 mL) finely chopped fresh herbs (use a combination of Italian parsley, basil, tarragon, chives, thyme, and oregano)
> Juice and zest of 1 lemon
> Salt and freshly ground black pepper, to taste
> Sprigs of fresh herbs

Place the chicken stock and lemon verbena leaves in a medium saucepan, and bring the stock to a simmer.

In a larger saucepan, heat the butter and olive oil over medium heat. Add the shallots and garlic and sauté until they are translucent and a very pale gold color.

Add the rice and sauté for 1–2 minutes. Add the stock, one ladleful at a time, stirring constantly. When each ladle of stock is absorbed, add another. Continue this for 18–20 minutes. The rice should be al dente, with a creamy consistency.

Stir in the Parmesan cheese, reserving 1 Tbsp. (15 mL) for garnish. Stir in the herbs, lemon juice and zest. Season with salt and pepper. Garnish with the herb sprigs and the reserved Parmesan cheese. If the risotto sits for a few minutes, add a little stock and fluff with a spoon just before serving.

Homemade Strawberry Ice Cream

Don't purée the strawberries—their texture adds that fresh strawberry quality to the ice cream. Serve it with a few whole berries and
the Mint Madeleines.

Makes approximately 4 cups (950 mL)

>   1⅓ cups (320 mL) milk
>   2⅔ cups (635 mL) heavy cream
>   ½ vanilla bean, split lengthwise
>   8 egg yolks
>   1¼ cups (300 mL) granulated sugar
>   2 cups (475 mL) fresh strawberries, rinsed, drained and stemmed

Combine the milk, cream and vanilla bean in a large heavy saucepan. Bring almost to a boil, reduce the heat and simmer gently for
5 minutes.

Whisk the egg yolks together with 1 cup (240 mL) of the sugar
until the mixture is smooth and the sugar has dissolved. Remove the
cream mixture from the heat and remove the vanilla bean. Whisk
1 cup (240 mL) of the hot cream thoroughly into the egg mixture.
Whisk the egg mixture back into the cream.

Return the saucepan to the stove and cook over low heat,
stirring constantly with a wooden spoon, just until the mixture
thickens. Do not boil. Strain, cool and chill well. Crush the strawberries with the remaining sugar and let sit for 20 minutes. Combine
the strawberries with the chilled custard. Transfer to an ice cream
maker and freeze according to the manufacturer's instructions.

Mint Madeleines

A delightful little shell-shaped French cake famous for its connection to Marcel Proust. I have adapted this recipe in order to simplify the more traditional, long-winded method, with help from the *David Wood Dessert Book*. Use a very light touch when incorporating the ingredients, as you would with muffins.

Makes 24 madeleines

> 1 cup (240 mL) unbleached all purpose flour
> ¼ tsp. (1.2 mL) salt
> ½ tsp. (2.5 mL) baking powder
> 2 large eggs
> ⅔ cup (160 mL) sugar
> 1 tsp. (5 mL) pure vanilla extract
> ½ cup (120 mL) plus 1 Tbsp. (15 mL) unsalted butter, melted
>   and cooled
> Zest of ½ lemon, finely chopped
> 2 Tbsp. (30 mL) fresh lemon juice
> 2 Tbsp. (30 mL) finely chopped fresh mint
> 2 Tbsp. (30 mL) icing sugar

Preheat the oven to 350°F (175°C). Butter and flour two madeleine molds.

Combine the flour, salt and baking powder in a bowl. Place the eggs, sugar and vanilla in a medium to large bowl, and beat over simmering water until doubled in volume. Remove from the heat and whisk until completely cool and almost doubled again in volume. (You can do this with an electric mixer.) The eggs should be creamy and light, with no large air bubbles.

Sift about half the flour mixture over the eggs, and fold gently until the flour has disappeared from the top of the batter. Drizzle some of the cool butter over the batter and fold it in. Alternate gently folding in the butter and flour until both are completely incorporated.

Fold in the lemon zest, juice and mint. Do not overmix. The lighter the batter, the fluffier the madeleines will be.

Spoon the batter into the molds, filling them ¾ full. Bake approximately 15–20 minutes, until golden brown.

Remove the madeleines from the pans right away and cool on a rack. When they are completely cool, turn them shell side up and dust with icing sugar. The madeleines will keep fresh for at least 2 days in an airtight container. They can be frozen for up to a month.

Asparagus Lover's Buffet

Asparagus and strawberries are two of my seasonal favorites. If you are a true asparagus lover, you'll delight in this all-out asparagus blitz. If you prefer a more moderate approach, choose one or two of these recipes and combine them with other dishes.

At Ravenhill we have access to an abundance of herbs and edible flowers. When a recipe calls for a garnish, use whatever you find esthetically pleasing from the herbs and edible flowers that are available to you.

Dolly's Asparagus Roll

Spicy Asparagus Maki Rolls

Asparagus and Basil Salad

Chilled Asparagus Soup with Fennel and Ewe's Milk Yogurt

Asparagus and Prawn Tart

Strawberries with Mint and Lemon Verbena

Dolly's Asparagus Roll

My grandmother Dolly used to make a similar roll, except that she used butter, cream cheese and canned asparagus! If you wish to make more sandwiches, cook more asparagus and double the cheese mixture. You can ask your local bakery to slice the bread lengthwise for you.

Makes approximately 20–24 pieces

12 asparagus spears, woody ends removed and discarded
8 oz. (225 g) chèvre (goat's milk cheese)
1 Tbsp. (15 mL) mayonnaise
2 Tbsp. (30 mL) finely chopped fresh tarragon
1 clove garlic, pressed
Salt and freshly ground black pepper, to taste
1 12-inch (30-cm) loaf very fresh white sandwich bread, sliced
    ½ inch (1.2 cm) thick lengthwise and crust removed
2 tsp. (10 mL) lemon juice
2–3 sprigs tarragon
1 Tbsp. (15 mL) chopped chives
2–3 edible flowers

Bring a large pot of salted water to a boil. Fill a large bowl with ice water and set it next to the stove. Blanch the spears for 3–4 minutes until tender but still crisp. Plunge into ice water until cool and set aside. (This method, which helps retain color and flavor, can be used for blanching other vegetables.)

Combine the cheese, mayonnaise, tarragon and garlic. Spread the mixture evenly over one long crustless slice. Place approximately 6 asparagus spears end to end along the slice of bread, just below the center. Season with salt and pepper and sprinkle 1 tsp. (5 mL) lemon juice over the asparagus. Firmly, but gently, roll up the bread lengthwise and secure. Slice the roll into ½-inch-thick (1.2-cm) slices. Repeat with another slice of bread. Place the rolls on a platter and decorate with tarragon sprigs and some chives and edible flower petals.

Spicy Asparagus Maki Rolls

Making sushi and maki rolls is very therapeutic and rewarding. Once you have the basic supplies on hand, it will encourage you to make maki rolls more often. Invest in a bamboo rolling mat, which is available at Asian food stores. Wasabi can also be purchased at Asian food stores in tube form or as a powder which is mixed with water to form a paste. Extra nori sheets can be stored in a dry, well-sealed container. Serve the rolls with sake.

Makes approximately 40 pieces

Juice of ½ lemon
1 Tbsp. (15 mL) sweet marjoram, finely chopped
Hot pepper sauce, to taste
½ cup (120 mL) mayonnaise
½ tsp. (2.5 mL) wasabi
2 cups (475 mL) raw short-grain Japanese rice
3–4 Tbsp. (45–60 mL) seasoned rice wine vinegar
1 1-oz. (28-g) package nori seaweed
½ cup (120 mL) toasted sesame seeds
2 cups (475 mL) packed arugula leaves or watercress
1 red bell pepper, thinly sliced
1 bunch fresh chives, or 6 green onions
10 asparagus spears, blanched (see page 83)
Nasturtium leaves and chive flowers
4 Tbsp. (60 mL) pickled ginger
1–2 Tbsp. (15–30 mL) wasabi

Combine the lemon juice, marjoram, hot sauce, mayonnaise and wasabi paste in a bowl. Taste for seasoning, cover and place in the refrigerator until ready to use.

Cook the rice according to directions, then transfer to a large bowl. Add the vinegar, cutting it in with a wooden spoon as the rice cools. Cover with a damp clean cloth until you're ready to use it.

Have a bowl of warm water beside you for rinsing your fingers while you are preparing the rolls. Lay the bamboo mat on the counter.

Cover it with a piece of plastic wrap. Place one sheet of nori on the plastic-covered mat, shiny side down. Dip your fingers in the warm water and place rice in a thin layer on the nori, covering about 90% of the sheet. Leave about ½ inch (1.2 cm) at the top edge. Spread a thin strip of the spicy mayonnaise mixture horizontally across the middle of the rice. Sprinkle with sesame seeds. Place some arugula leaves horizontally across the middle and sprinkle with some red pepper. Lay some chives or green onions and 2 asparagus spears, with their tips facing outwards, across the middle of the rice.

Start to roll from the bottom edge closest to you, using the bamboo mat to help you tuck in the filling as you roll. Just before you finish rolling, slightly moisten the bare nori at the end of the roll with a little mayonnaise. Finish rolling, squeeze the roll gently with the mat to ensure it is tightly sealed, and remove the mat. Repeat until all the rice is used up. Wrap the rolls in plastic and chill until ready to slice.

Slice each roll into approximately 8 pieces, each ½–¾ inch (1.2–2 cm) thick. Dip a sharp knife in water, and wipe it off between slices. Slice at a slight angle. Decorate with nasturtium leaves and chive flowers. Serve with soy sauce, pickled ginger and extra wasabi.

Asparagus and Basil Salad

This salad can be served as a simple side dish with any main course.

Serves 4–6

> 12 asparagus spears, blanched and cooled (see page 83)
> 1 cup (240 mL) packed fresh basil, julienned
> ¼ cup (60 mL) extra virgin olive oil
> 1½ Tbsp. (22.5 mL) balsamic vinegar
> 2 shallots, finely chopped
> Salt and freshly ground black pepper, to taste

Toss all the ingredients together and let marinate about 15 minutes before serving.

Chilled Asparagus Soup with Fennel and Ewe's Milk Yogurt

This soup also complements the Herbal Tea Party menu (page 112). If desired, blanch some extra asparagus tips for garnish. Ewe's milk yogurt is deliciously rich and not as pungent as goat's milk products. It is available at most large food markets. You can substitute a good-quality cow's milk yogurt.

Serves 4–6

> 2 Tbsp. (30 mL) butter
> 4 shallots, finely chopped
> 4 cloves garlic, finely chopped
> 4 cups (950 mL) hot chicken stock
> 12 asparagus spears, blanched and cooled (see page 83)
> 2 Tbsp. (30 mL) ewe's milk yogurt
> Salt and freshly ground black pepper, to taste
> 2 Tbsp. (30 mL) finely chopped fennel fronds

Melt the butter in a large soup pot over medium heat. Add the shallots and garlic and sauté for 3–4 minutes, until translucent. Add the chicken stock and asparagus and simmer until the asparagus is soft enough to purée.

Remove from the heat and purée until smooth. Place a medium serving bowl into a larger bowl of ice. Strain the soup through a fine mesh strainer into the serving bowl. Whisk the yogurt into the strained soup, season to taste and sprinkle with fennel. Chill and serve.

Asparagus and Prawn Tart

With a crisp green salad and a good white wine, this tart makes a delicious lunch.

Serves 8 generously

½ cup (120 mL) dry white wine or vermouth
1 bay leaf
1 tsp. (5 mL) whole peppercorns, black or mixed
Salt, to taste
12 fresh medium-size prawns
4 eggs
¼ cup (60 mL) whipping cream
½ cup (120 mL) finely chopped fresh chives
Salt and freshly ground black pepper, to taste
2 Tbsp. (30 mL) finely chopped fresh Italian or curly parsley
16 asparagus spears, blanched and cooled (see page 83)
Prebaked tart shell (use the Rhubarb Tart pastry recipe on page 53 but omit the sugar)

Preheat the oven to 350°F (175°C).

In a medium saucepan combine the wine, bay leaf and peppercorns. Season with a pinch of salt. Bring to a simmer, add the prawns, and blanch until they just turn pink, approximately 5 minutes. Remove from the heat and let cool in the stock.

In a medium bowl, whisk together the eggs, cream and chives until well mixed. Season with salt and pepper. Peel the prawns and toss them in 1 Tbsp. (15 mL) of the parsley. Scatter the asparagus and prawns evenly over the tart shell and cover with the egg mixture.

Bake for approximately 20–25 minutes until lightly golden. Sprinkle with the remaining parsley and cool for 10 minutes before slicing.

Strawberries with Mint and Lemon Verbena

After such an asparagus indulgence, these fresh strawberries will clean your palate and aid digestion, finishing this menu beautifully. This dessert can be made a few hours ahead.

Serves 4–6

> 4 cups (950 mL) fresh strawberries, gently washed and hulled
> 2 tsp. (10 mL) fresh lemon juice
> 1 tsp. (5 mL) finely chopped fresh lemon verbena
> 1 Tbsp. (15 mL) finely chopped fresh mint
> ½ tsp. (2.5 mL) minced fresh ginger
> 1 Tbsp. (15 mL) sugar
> 1 Tbsp. (15 mL) finely chopped fennel fronds

Toss all the ingredients together and serve in individual glasses or in one large glass bowl.

July
and
August

Summer: Birds, Basil
and Barbecues

Dining is and always was a great artistic opportunity.
——FRANK LLOYD WRIGHT

Lettuce is divine, although I'm not sure it's really a food.
——DIANA VREELAND

The best sauce in the whole world is hunger.

——CERVANTES

Without bread all is misery.

——WILLIAM COBBETT

PEOPLE MEASURE AND DIVIDE their lives in various ways: by literary coffee spoons, by seasons, decades, various passions or relationships, marriages or other exciting events. I measure my life by summers. I think back on all the summers I have had and where I spent them, and then my mind tries to contemplate how many I may have left to enjoy.

This focus on summer probably began because both my parents were teachers. Summer changed everything. My parents relaxed and so did all the children. Five army cots were put outside my parents' bedroom windows and we children all moved out of the house for the duration of good weather. If we sang, or giggled or talked too much during the night, my father would stick his head out the window and roar, "If I hear one more word, you will all come in and sleep inside." This silenced us quickly, for we loved sleeping outside, listening to the night noises and scaring ourselves silly.

At Ravenhill Farm, July begins with the garden looking glorious, especially if we have had a rainy June. The lavender is almost at its peak. From the kitchen window I can see the pinkish-orange alstromeria and the lavender bushes merging into a great mauve-pink cloud. If I squint, this scene blurs into a vision as beautiful as a Monet painting. (I once saw this artist's thick spectacles in a museum in Paris. As he aged, Monet's poor eyesight influenced his fuzzy, soft-edged paintings.)

Down the path beyond the lavender, I can see the fennel forest reaching up to almost 6 feet (2 metres) in height. Its lime-green foliage and yellow flower umbels stand out against the old, dark green Douglas firs at the edge of the garden. If we get a stretch of hot weather, the meadows start turning a parched, African-veldt yellow, and parts of the garden start to shrivel by late July. Our water is provided by two mediocre wells, so we have to accept this. I dream of sprinkling systems and green luxuriance. Instead there are small oases where we're able to water.

My potted plants flourish on the patio. Great branches of lemon verbena, myrtle and rosemary fill the air with scent; they must be watered every day, or they'll swoon and droop in the heat.

At this time of year I cruise the country roads with a basket, looking at what other people are growing and selling at their roadside stands. The roads are lined with the palest blue chicory flowers and creamy white Queen Anne's lace. No designer florist could dream up a more perfect combination. The municipality's machines maniacally trim and cut the wildflowers and grasses by the roadside, but they cannot defeat the amazing energy of these weeds. Bloom they will. Let us hope the powers-that-be never resort to poison to control these beautiful country flowers.

On my road there is a flower stand with bouquets by Effie. She arranges them beautifully, and with one swoop there are flowers to fill all the rooms. I like her caustic notes to people who steal her flowers without paying. "You know who you are," she writes. Farther down I find sweet peas, corn and enormous sunflowers at Robert's stand. I love to have sunflower bouquets on the old, gray patio table. One of my favorite flower signs is "Fresh Booquets." I can gather tomatoes, corn and organic blue-berries close by, and on Saturdays we go to the market at the fairgrounds, which each year has more produce, unique crafts, food and music. I return happily home with laden baskets.

Our meadows are mowed every July by a neighbor, Jamie. He lived in our house when he was a child and knows every bump in the fields. The mouse nests are destroyed by haying, and the mice run for cover, hungrily watched by crows and ravens circling above. Everyone hopes it does not rain the night after cutting. With luck, the hay is tedded (tossed over to dry) and baled in the next few days. The fields suddenly look tidy, yellow and groomed. In late September, when the autumn rains begin, a tinge of green will appear and the grass will grow again, making the sheep happier.

We often have lots of guests in the summer, and there are special meals I like to prepare to celebrate their visits and the season. One is "The Big Grill." We often celebrate July 1st, 4th, or Bastille Day by having a barbecue with some friends. Flank steak or butterflied leg of lamb are favorite things to grill. I begin marinating them the day before with lots of herbs and freshly harvested garlic. Once I flung a bunch of cilantro on some flank steak, added chopped garlic and a dash of soy sauce and left it overnight. The meat was beautifully perfumed.

Many vegetables, such as tomatoes, mushrooms, squash, zucchini and green onions, are enhanced by grilling. Aïoli, the "butter of Provence" made with new garlic, is wonderful with grilled food. It has true garlic fire and power, and makes store-bought mayonnaise seem like a tepid second cousin.

Raspberries and ice cream are the perfect no-fuss ending to this meal. Send any children or twitchy guests out to pick the raspberries. This clears the decks while you are cooking. One summer I became the ultimate lazy dessert cook. I leaned back after dinner and asked my well-fed guests if they wanted dessert. They smiled expectantly, and then I dropped the bombshell. "Go and pick yellow plums in the garden," I said. This sounded slightly rude, but really I was offering them the lovely experience of wandering through the garden at dusk to pick and eat oozy, juicy, yellow plums and watch the moon rise over the valley.

Jenny and I have done a basil/garlic dinner, redolent with flavor, several times for a cooking class. Surprisingly, although there is basil and/or garlic in everything, the flavors are not overwhelming. The freshly harvested garlic has sweet overtones, with none of the bitterness associated with winter storage. Freshly picked basil appears in the appetizer pizza, the flank steak marinade, the aïoli, the pesto sauce, the tomato salad and my favorite, the ice cream, which is very subtle. For some reason guests always seem to get a little hilarious at this perfumed meal. I think it is the amazing fragrances of the basil and garlic, and not the wine at all. At the last basil/garlic class there were a great variety of people of all ages and professions, including English academics, a magazine publisher, and blueberry farmers bearing the fruits of their fields. The just-picked blueberries were sprinkled onto the chartreuse-green basil ice cream, making a color combination a decorator would die for.

The last two summer menus are a herbal tea party and a crab feast. We have done the tea party as a total herbal experience that takes all of one sunny afternoon. Sometimes groups ferry over from Vancouver for this class. First, guests are served an exquisite array of open-face sandwiches, completely decorated and flavored with herbs. Smoked salmon with chives, egg salad with tarragon, basil cream cheese, cucumber with shrimp and dill, tomato basil, and crab with fennel. The cookies are laced with lemon verbena, lemon balm and mint, as is the tea I make in the giant 20-cupper I found in Chinatown. Sometimes we make a lavender cake or rose-petal ice cream. The guests can wander through the garden, gaze at the view of the valley and the sea and buy plants if they wish. They return home sated with herbal scents, herbal tastes and sunshine. It has never turned out to be a rainy day when we've offered this class!

The crab feast is one of my favorite ways of entertaining. Also it is one of the easiest and the most impressive ways to please your guests. I count the number of guests, and then drive to the Satellite Fish Shop on the Sidney wharf. If the crabs have just been cooked that is fine, but I like to get them live if possible (one per person). I rush home with the live crabs, put a large kettle on to boil, and throw a generous handful of tarragon in the pot.

I boil the crabs for about 18 minutes. This process is not for the squeamish. If you are one of those, then buy the crabs cooked. I push them down into the water with a long wooden spoon and thank them for providing me with such a delicious meal. They usually die gracefully, although sometimes they scramble to get out. I wear large oven mitts so I won't get pinched.

I mix up a cocktail sauce with horseradish, mayonnaise, fresh chives, ketchup and lemon juice. I melt butter with lots of fresh lemon juice and place it in several small bowls around the table. We serve the crab with plenty of crusty bread and a plain green salad. We put out lots of napkins and finger bowls of warm water with floating lemon verbena leaves, because eating crab is a joyous, juicy, messy experience. Crack the crab with a mallet before placing it on a platter, fling some parsley and lemon wedges over it and make a grand entrance holding the platter aloft. This is truly a special, festive way to end the summer.

Images of summer often remain in my memory. This summer a Japanese plum tree that had seeded itself on the driveway bore a huge crop of plums. The ravens and their new family descended from the tall Douglas firs where they usually reside and began to eat the scarlet fruit. About 20 ravens gathered around the tree in the yellow field and happily gobbled the plums. The sight of a black raven flying by with the brilliant red fruit in its beak was truly amazing. It looked like an illustration from an old fairy tale.

After a week or so the birds had finished harvesting the tree and moved into the next meadow to eat the pale yellow transparent apples. This fruit gathering is always accompanied by much raven chatter, cawing and guttural, gobbling noises. The birds have quite a conversational repertoire. Sometimes when I do not have an audience I imitate them and they call back to me. What are they thinking? Are they thinking, "Does this strange creature know what she is saying to us?" I am glad we named the farm Ravenhill after the ravens, and I understand why First Nations people include this wily, clever bird in their lives and legends.

Another sign from the birds: about five o'clock every evening the Canada geese appear in great flocks. They circle around the valley, then head out to Brentwood Bay where they spend the night. It is intriguing to think that the geese are repeating a pattern they have been recreating for centuries, long before European pioneers started settling here in the late 1850s. Their honking and the noise of their rushing wings as they fly over remind me that summer is coming to an end.

The Big Grill

The keys to success with this and other barbecues are great marinades and fresh produce. Proficiency at the grill and, of course, good company, are also important. This menu is suggested for a group of eight or more, but it may also be done on a smaller scale with a few chosen vegetables and less lamb.

Grilled Stuffed Grape Leaves with Green Grape
and Basil Salsa

Grilled Butterfly Leg of Lamb "Au Vin"

Grilled Vegetables with Worldly Flavors

Fresh Raspberries with Lemon Verbena Cream

Grilled Stuffed Grape Leaves
with Green Grape Basil Salsa

At Ravenhill we have a beautiful old grapevine, and when the leaves are still young, this is a favorite starter to any menu.

Makes 12

12 fresh, young grape vine leaves, stems removed
½ cup (60 mL) olive oil
2 small rounds of ewe's milk Camembert, each cut into 6 wedges
¼ cup (60 mL) finely chopped fresh chives
Freshly ground black pepper, to taste
1 recipe Green Grape and Basil Salsa (page 98)

Preheat the grill to medium. Presoak 12 toothpicks.

Bring a medium saucepan of salted water to a simmer. Blanch the grape leaves, 2 to 3 at a time, for approximately 1 minute. Gently remove and separate the leaves, placing each leaf shiny side down on a clean tea towel. Pat them dry and brush each leaf with olive oil. Place one wedge of cheese on each leaf. Sprinkle with chives and pepper. Tuck the vine leaf around the cheese, rolling away from you, and folding in the sides until you have a snug little parcel. Brush lightly with olive oil.

Repeat until all the grape leaves are stuffed and parceled. Spear each with a toothpick to keep the bundle together while cooking and serving. Grill for approximately 2 minutes per side. Serve immediately with the Green Grape and Basil Salsa.

Green Grape and Basil Salsa

Makes approximately 1 cup (240 mL)

½ lb. (225 g) green seedless grapes, finely
    chopped
2 Tbsp. (30 mL) finely chopped fresh basil
1 shallot, finely chopped
1 tsp. (5 mL) extra virgin olive oil
½ tsp. (2.5 mL) white wine vinegar or
    champagne vinegar
Salt and freshly ground pepper, to taste

Combine all the ingredients and taste for seasoning. (If you prefer the salsa slightly sweeter, add a pinch of sugar.)

Let the salsa sit for at least 15 minutes. Serve with stuffed grapevine leaves.

Bay

The leaves that formed the victors' garlands in the Olympic games of ancient Greece came from the noble bay. It happily survives in our colder climate as a bush or small tree planted on the west side of a house.

Grilled Butterflied Leg of Lamb "Au Vin"

This recipe of mine appeared in *Sunset* magazine in July 1999. The marinade is also excellent with barbecued flank steak.

Serves 6–8

    1 6- to 8-lb. (2.7- to 3.6-kg) leg of lamb, boned and butterflied
    ½ cup (120 mL) extra virgin olive oil
    2 cups (475 mL) red wine
    ¾ cup (180 mL) soy sauce
    3 large cloves garlic, finely chopped or pressed
    1 large bunch cilantro, coarsely chopped, reserving a few sprigs
        for garnish
    2 bay leaves
    Coarse sea salt and freshly ground black pepper, to taste

Place the lamb in a large roasting dish. Combine the remaining ingredients and pour over the lamb, turning it several times to ensure it is well coated. Cover in plastic wrap and refrigerate 4–24 hours (the longer the better), turning every few hours.

Oil the grill and place the rack 4–6 inches (10–15 cm) above the heat source. Preheat the barbecue to hot. Place the lamb on the grill and sear each side for 10 minutes. Brush with marinade each time you turn the lamb. For medium rare, continue grilling over medium heat, turning and basting for another 20–30 minutes. For medium, add 15 minutes. Thicker parts of the lamb will be pink and thin parts will be more cooked, so you can please everybody. Let the lamb rest for 10–15 minutes on a warm platter before carving. Decorate with sprigs of fresh cilantro.

- Clean and lightly oil the grill with a clean rag before turning it on.

- Preheat the grill for at least 10 minutes with the lid closed before starting.

- Have a serving platter with decorative herbs and flowers ready for the cooked food.

- Use good-quality, elbow-length oven mitts, and stainless steel tongs and flipper.

- Meat marinades should be boiled for at least 5 minutes before using them as a sauce. This destroys any harmful bacteria. When basting meats on the grill, make sure the raw marinade is cooked before serving.

Grilled Vegetables with Worldly Flavors

There is a wide array of vegetables that are great done on the barbecue. I have suggested marinades that would suit each vegetable, but the menu is completely flexible. The amounts you cook will depend on the number of diners at your table. Add good-quality olives, artichoke hearts and marinated chickpeas to the platter of grilled vegetables before serving.

Grill the vegetables over a preheated barbecue set on medium. The cooking times are approximate, depending on the size of the pieces and the heat of the barbecue. Once the vegetables are done, brush them with more marinade.

Baby Bok Choy or Sui Choy

Split into halves or quarters depending on the size. Brush lightly with marinade and grill 2–3 minutes per side. Marinade suggestions: Chinese, Thai or Southwestern.

Carrots

Peel and slice them in half widthwise, and then in quarters lengthwise, so the pieces are flat. Blanch for 2–3 minutes in simmering water. Lightly brush with marinade and grill for 2–3 minutes per side until just tender. Marinade suggestions: Spanish, Greek or French.

Eggplant

Slice into ¼- to ½-inch (.6- to 1.2-cm) rings. Salt lightly and place between paper towels for 15 minutes. Blot with paper towels and brush lightly with marinade. Grill 3–4 minutes per side. Marinade suggestions: Italian, Chinese or Indian. (Note: When using the Indian marinade, lightly brush the eggplant with olive oil before grilling and toss with the marinade when done.)

Fennel Bulb

Cut in quarters lengthwise, so that the pieces are flat, keeping the root intact. Brush lightly with marinade and grill 3–4 minutes per side. Marinade suggestions: Italian, Greek or French.

Green Onion

Trim the ends and grill whole for 1–2 minutes. Marinade suggestions: Chinese or Thai.

Mushrooms

Grill whole for 3–4 minutes, head down. Turn and grill for 2 minutes more. Marinade suggestions: Italian, Chinese or Southwestern.

Marinades

The liquid ingredients in each recipe form the base for each marinade. Create your own tastes, bearing in mind that acid (vinegar or lemon juice) and oil should be balanced. There should be roughly ¼ cup (60 mL) of acidic liquid to ⅔–1 cup (160–240 mL) of oil.

Chinese
Soy sauce, rice wine vinegar, sesame oil (use sparingly), olive oil, grated ginger, garlic, cilantro. Optional: hoisin sauce, sambal oelek, chilies, five-spice powder, orange juice, green onion.

French
Tarragon, white wine vinegar, dry white vermouth, garlic, shallots, olive oil. Optional: chervil, lemon juice, salt and pepper, chives.

Greek
Extra virgin olive oil, red wine vinegar or lemon juice, garlic, thyme, oregano, salt and pepper. Optional: mint, anchovy paste.

Marinades (cont.)

Indian
Plain yogurt, lemon or lime juice, plus ground cumin, coriander or curry powder, and fresh mint. Optional: fresh cilantro, grated ginger, ground cardamom, chives.

Italian
Extra virgin olive oil, balsamic vinegar, garlic, basil, salt and pepper. Optional: rosemary, Dijon mustard, sun-dried tomatoes, olive paste.

Southwestern
Extra virgin olive oil, lime juice, cumin and chili powder. Optional: tomato paste, fresh cilantro.

Spanish
Dijon mustard, brown sugar, sherry, olive oil, lemon juice, fresh thyme, garlic, salt and pepper.

Thai
Soy sauce, peanut butter, olive oil, sesame oil (use sparingly), rice wine vinegar, lime juice, basil and chili peppers. Optional: fish sauce (nam pla).

Peppers

Slice red, green and yellow sweet peppers in half lengthwise and remove the seeds. Brush lightly with marinade. Grill 3–4 minutes per side until just tender. Slice the halves into quarters after they are cooked. Marinade suggestions: Greek or Italian.

Potatoes

Slice ½ inch (1.2 cm) thick. Parboil in simmering water for 4–5 minutes. Dry well, lightly brush with marinade and grill 5–6 minutes per side. Marinade suggestions: Italian, Greek or French.

Radicchio

Split into quarters. Lightly brush with marinade and grill cut side down for 1–2 minutes. Marinade suggestions: Italian or Chinese.

Romaine Lettuce

Remove the large outer leaves and split into quarters. Brush lightly with marinade, and grill, cut side down, for 1–2 minutes. Marinade suggestions: Italian, with a sprinkle of Parmesan cheese at the end.

Shallots and Garlic

Peel and grill whole. Lightly brush with marinade. Use a lightly oiled, fine-mesh vegetable grate to prevent these small vegetables from falling through. Move them about to prevent burning and grill for 6–10 minutes. Marinade suggestions: Italian, Greek or Southwestern.

Tomatoes

Cut larger tomatoes in half. Grill cherry tomatoes whole. Use a lightly oiled, fine-mesh vegetable grate. Brush lightly with marinade and grill skin side down for 1–2 minutes. Marinade suggestions: Italian or Greek.

Zucchini

Slice on a slight diagonal into rings ½ inch (1.2 cm) thick. Grill 2–3 minutes per side. Marinade suggestions: Greek, French or Italian.

Grilling Bread

Grilled bread is a great addition to any meal where you've fired up the barbecue. Use a robust, crusty sourdough or baguette for grilling. Slice it ½ inch (1.2 cm) thick, brush it lightly with an Italian or French marinade and grill it 1–2 minutes per side.

Fresh Raspberries with Lemon Verbena Cream

Lemon Verbena

This tender shrub needs the warmest, sunniest spot in the garden, preferably against a south-facing house or wall. We bring ours into a cool greenhouse for the winter and set them out on the patio in April.

At Ravenhill, we pick raspberries from the garden after dinner when they are in season.

Serves 4–6

> 1 Tbsp. (15 mL) finely chopped fresh lemon verbena
> Zest and juice of 1 lemon
> ¼ cup (60 mL) sugar
> 2 cups (475 mL) fresh whipping cream
> 4–6 cups (950 mL–1.5 L) fresh raspberries

Combine the lemon verbena, lemon zest and juice and sugar in a small saucepan. Cook over medium heat until the mixture gently bubbles and the sugar dissolves. Strain and let cool.

Whip the cream and add the lemon mixture halfway through whipping.

Divide the raspberries between 4–6 wine glasses and top with the lemon whipped cream.

Basil and Garlic Dinner

The warm days of summer are here, and it's time to sing the praises of basil and garlic, which flavor our meals all summer at the farm. The basil/garlic beat goes on until the cool days of fall arrive.

Thin Crust Pizza with Roasted Garlic, Fresh Basil, Blue Cheese and Pear Zest

Barbecued Flank Steak Marinated with Basil and Garlic

Steamed New Potatoes with Basil Pesto

Tomato Salad with Basil, Feta and Capers

Basil Ice Cream with Bitter Chocolate Sauce

Thin Crust Pizza with Roasted Garlic, Fresh Basil, Blue Cheese and Pear Zest

This is a summery pizza, rich with basil and roasted garlic. Serve it with robust red wine or a fruity white wine, such as Chardonnay. The pizza crust is made with Noël's French bread dough, which appeared in her book *Winter Pleasures*. Use half the dough for the pizza and either freeze the other half or use it to make bread or buns.

Makes 10–12 slices

For the pizza crust:

½ cup (120 mL) warm water
1 tsp. (5 mL) sugar
¼ tsp. (1.2 mL) ground ginger
2 Tbsp. (30 mL) dry yeast
5 cups (1.2 L) unbleached white flour
2 cups (475 mL) warm water
2 Tbsp. (30 mL) sugar
1½ tsp. (7.5 mL) salt
2 Tbsp. (30 mL) olive oil
¼ cup (60 mL) finely chopped sage, rosemary or herb of your
    choice (optional)
1 cup (240 mL) flour

Combine the ½ cup (120 mL) warm water, 1 tsp. (5 mL) sugar, ginger and yeast in a bowl and let stand until bubbling well, about 10 minutes. (The addition of ginger improves the yeast.)

Place the 5 cups (1.2 L) flour in a large mixing bowl and make a well in the middle of the flour. Put the 2 cups (475 mL) warm water, the bubbling yeast mixture and the 2 Tbsp. (30 mL) sugar in the depression. Mix enough flour into the yeast mixture to slightly thicken it. Let stand for about 20 minutes. The yeast mixture will mound up and bubble in the center.

Add the salt and oil and the herbs, if desired, and stir in the rest of the flour in the bowl. Mix well with a wooden spoon; the dough will be stiff.

Put the last cup (240 mL) flour on a smooth surface and turn out the dough. Knead firmly and with energy for 10 minutes. Set the timer so you do not cheat. When done, the dough should form a smooth, non-sticky ball. Lightly oil the bowl and the dough and replace the dough in the bowl. Cover with a clean cloth and let rise for at least 2 hours, until doubled in size.

Punch down the dough. (If you're making bread, let it rise again for another hour until doubled.) Divide the dough into 2 balls. Use 1 ball for the pizza. Either freeze the other one for another pizza or use it to make loaves or baguettes.

On a lightly floured counter, roll one ball of dough out thinly, until it is ¼–½ inch (.6–1.2 cm) thick. Place it on a preheated pizza stone or pizza pan.

To make the pizza:

1 bulb garlic, separated and peeled
¼ cup (60 mL) extra virgin olive oil
1 Tbsp. (15 mL) balsamic vinegar
Salt and freshly ground black pepper, to taste
1 cup (240 mL) julienned fresh basil leaves
2 ripe or poached pears, peeled and cooled
1 cup (240 mL) blue cheese, such as Danish blue or Stilton

Preheat the oven to 475°F (250°C).

Combine the garlic, olive oil, balsamic vinegar, salt and pepper in a small ovenproof dish. Cover in foil and roast for 15–20 minutes. Remove the foil and roast for another 10–15 minutes. Put the garlic and basil in a food processor, reserving 1 Tbsp. (15 mL) basil for garnish, and purée until smooth.

Spread the garlic basil purée over the pizza dough. Using a zester or a grater, zest or grate the flesh of the pears and sprinkle it over the purée. Top with the blue cheese. Place in the oven for approximately 15 minutes, until the crust is crispy. Cut into small wedges and sprinkle with the reserved basil.

Barbecued Flank Steak Marinated with Basil and Garlic

My very favorite steak for summer grilling. The basil and garlic are massaged into the meat for a rich flavor sensation. Serve the flank steak with Basil Aïoli (page 132).

Serves 6

> 1 bulb garlic, cloves separated, peeled and finely chopped or pressed
> 2 cups (475 mL) fresh basil, finely chopped
> 2 lb. (900 g) flank steak
> ½ cup (120 mL) extra virgin olive oil
> 1 cup (240 mL) red wine
> Salt and freshly ground black pepper, to taste

Combine the garlic and basil and rub the flank steak on all sides with the mixture. Add the olive oil, red wine, salt and pepper. Marinate for a few hours or overnight, turning occasionally.

Preheat the grill to high. Grill the flank steak for 5 minutes per side initially, basting as you turn the meat. Turn the heat down to medium and cook another 4–5 minutes per side for medium-rare. If you prefer rare meat, cook it for a shorter time; cook longer for medium to well done. The cooking time will vary depending on the thickness and weight of the meat. Let the meat rest for 10 minutes before slicing. Slice it very thinly, against the grain, for maximum tenderness.

Steamed New Potatoes with Basil Pesto

Clean and prepare the potatoes, preferably local new potatoes, allowing 3 or 4 per person, depending on the size. Steam for approximately 15 minutes until tender. Serve the pesto sauce on the side, or toss the potatoes lightly in the pesto and serve extra on the side.

Basil Pesto

This basil pesto is from Noël's book *Summer Delights*. Basil pesto is now firmly entrenched as a summer classic, but it freezes well, and you can enjoy it all winter on pasta or crackers and add it to soups and sauces for increased flavor.

Makes 2 cups (475 mL)

> 2 cups (475 mL) firmly packed basil leaves, freshly washed
> 2–4 cloves garlic, peeled and crushed
> ½ cup (120 mL) olive or vegetable oil
> 3 Tbsp. (45 mL) pine nuts
> 1 cup (240 mL) freshly grated Parmesan cheese

Put the basil and garlic in a blender or food processor. Pour in the oil and process until smooth. Add the pine nuts and process for a few seconds. Stir in the Parmesan cheese. If the sauce is too thick, add more oil. Store in a jar in the refrigerator with a skim of oil on top and cover with plastic wrap.

To freeze, place the pesto in plastic cartons and label. To use, thaw it slowly at room temperature. You can omit the pine nuts and cheese when processing and add them to the thawed pesto just before serving for a fresh taste.

Basil

Growing basil successfully in coastal B.C. is mainly a matter of providing adequate heat. Simple, clear plastic tunnels, 2 feet (60 cm) high, are adequate for protecting seedlings planted out at the end of April. The cover can be removed in mid-June or earlier if the plants get too large. Create ventilation by lifting one side on hot days, or by cutting a few small holes in the top of the tunnel. Basil's other requirements are rich, fast-draining soil and water every three days in hot weather.

Tomato Salad with Basil, Feta and Capers

This salad has a brave, gutsy flavor that marries well with barbecued meats.

Serves 4–6

6 fully ripe medium tomatoes
2 cups (475 mL) lettuce leaves, basil or other greens
¼ cup (60 mL) high-quality extra virgin olive oil
1½ Tbsp. (22.5 mL) balsamic vinegar
1 cup (240 mL) fresh basil, julienned
1 cup (240 mL) crumbled or cubed feta cheese
¼ cup (60 mL) capers
Salt and freshly ground black pepper, to taste

Slice the tomatoes and arrange them on a bed of greens. Drizzle with olive oil and balsamic vinegar. Sprinkle with the julienned basil. Top with the feta and capers. Season to taste with salt and pepper.

Basil Ice Cream with Bitter Chocolate Sauce

This recipe also appears in *Summer Delights*, but it is such a favorite, it's worth repeating.

Makes 2–2 ½ cups (475–600 mL)

> 2 cups (475 mL) milk
> ½ vanilla bean, split lengthwise
> 1 cup (240 mL) basil leaves
> 4 egg yolks
> 1 cup (240 mL) sugar

Bring the milk, vanilla bean and basil to a boil in a medium saucepan. Remove from the heat, cover, and let steep for 10–15 minutes.

In a large bowl, whisk the egg yolks and sugar until thick and creamy. Pour the milk and basil mixture into the egg and sugar mixture. Whisk well.

Pour into a saucepan, and cook over low heat. Stir constantly with a wooden spoon for 5–7 minutes. Strain and cool. Freeze in an ice cream maker, following the manufacturer's directions.

Bitter Chocolate Sauce

Makes 1 cup (240 mL)

> 4 oz. (113 g) unsweetened chocolate
> 2 Tbsp. (30 mL) butter
> 2 Tbsp. (30 mL) white corn syrup
> 6–8 Tbsp. (90–120 mL) sugar
> ¾ cup (180 mL) milk
> Pinch of salt

Melt the chocolate and butter over hot water. Blend in the corn syrup and sugar. Add the milk and salt. Cook over low heat for 10 minutes, stirring constantly. Serve warm or cool on ice cream.

Herbal Tea Party

An elegant "hold your pinkie out" party for a warm summer afternoon.

Cool Berry Soup

Open-Faced Tea Sandwiches

Mint Shortbread with Chocolate Drizzle

Lemon Thyme, Rose Petal, and Lavender Glazed Tea Cake

Lemon Verbena Iced Tea

Cool Berry Soup

Tastes like strawberry wine.

Serves 4–6

> 2 cups (475 mL) fresh strawberries or raspberries
> ½ cup (120 mL) sugar (use more or less to taste)
> ½ cup (120 mL) low-fat sour cream or high-quality plain yogurt
> ½ cup (120 mL) red wine
> 1½–2 cups (360–475 mL) ice water
> Edible flowers, such as johnny jump-ups or borage, for garnish

Rub the berries through a fine sieve. Add sugar to taste and sour cream or yogurt. Mix well. Add the wine, then add the water, a bit at a time. It should have the consistency of a smoothie, not too watery. Correct the sweetening and chill well before serving.

Open-Faced Tea Sandwiches

If you lightly butter each sandwich, it will help the ingredients adhere to the bread. Each recipe makes 8 sandwiches.

Fennel and Crab

> 8 oz. (225 g) Dungeness crabmeat
> 2 Tbsp. (30 mL) finely chopped fresh fennel fronds
> ½ tsp. (2.5 mL) lemon juice
> ½ tsp. (2.5 mL) horseradish
> 1 Tbsp. (15 mL) mayonnaise
> Salt and freshly ground pepper, to taste
> ½ white baguette, cut into 8 slices
> 8 sprigs fennel

Combine all the ingredients but the bread and fennel sprigs. Divide the filling equally among the baguette slices. Top each with a sprig of fennel.

Tarragon and Egg Salad

4 free-range eggs, hard-boiled and finely
    chopped
2 Tbsp. (30 mL) finely chopped fresh tarragon,
    and a bit extra for garnish
1 tsp. (5 mL) Dijon mustard
½ tsp. (2.5 mL) hot pepper sauce
2 Tbsp. (30 mL) mayonnaise
½ tsp. (2.5 mL) lemon juice
Salt and freshly ground black pepper, to taste
8 slices high-quality, very fresh white bread
1 small head butter lettuce, or 1 bunch watercress
Edible flower petals, for garnish

Combine the eggs, tarragon (reserving a bit for garnish), mustard, hot pepper sauce, mayonnaise, lemon juice, salt and pepper in a medium bowl.

Cut the center out of each slice of bread with a round or fluted 3-inch (7.5-cm) cookie or biscuit cutter. Place a small piece of lettuce or watercress on each bread round, and place approximately 1½ Tbsp. (22.5 mL) of egg salad on top. Decorate with a sprinkle of tarragon and some edible flower petals.

Edible Flowers

If you've never had a flower in your soup or salad, start by trying the individual florets of a chive blossom, then the petals of the nasturtium. Both have a stronger and more distinctive flavor than most edible flowers. Other edible flowers to try: borage, calendula, squash, marigold, violet, lavender, carnation and rose. Many of these have a lot of eye appeal and little for the palate.

Dill, Shrimp and Cucumber

8 oz. (225 g) fresh hand-peeled shrimp
2 Tbsp. (30 mL) finely chopped fresh dill, and a bit extra for garnish
½ tsp. (2.5 mL) lemon juice
Salt and freshly ground black pepper, to taste
4 oz. (113 g) cream cheese
1 clove garlic, pressed
½ white baguette, cut into 8 slices
8 thin slices of cucumber
Edible flower petals

Combine the shrimp, 1 Tbsp. (15 mL) of the dill, the lemon juice, salt and pepper. Cover and refrigerate. In a small bowl, combine the cream cheese, the remaining dill, and the garlic. Mix until smooth and creamy. Spread the cream cheese on each slice of bread. Put a slice of cucumber on one half of each slice, and place some of the shrimp mixture on the other half. Decorate with the extra dill and edible flower petals.

Chives and Smoked Salmon

1 Tbsp. (15 mL) capers
4 oz. (113 g) cream cheese
3 Tbsp. (45 mL) finely chopped fresh chives
1 shallot, finely chopped
8 small slices pumpernickel or rye bread
8 thin slices smoked salmon, preferably lox
½ tsp. (2.5 mL) lemon juice
Freshly ground black pepper, to taste

Combine half the capers, the cream cheese, 1 Tbsp. (15 mL) of the fresh chives and the shallot. Mix well. Spread the mixture on the bread. Place a slice of salmon on top, rolled into a decorative shape. Sprinkle with lemon juice and the remaining chives and capers. Top with a little grind of pepper.

Basil and Tomato

1 tsp. (5 mL) balsamic vinegar
1 Tbsp. (15 mL) extra virgin olive oil
½ tsp. (2.5 mL) Dijon mustard
Salt and freshly ground pepper to taste
3 Tbsp. (45 mL) fresh basil, finely julienned
½ white or sourdough baguette, cut into 8 slices
8 thin slices bocconcini mozzarella (approximately 2 balls)
8 cherry tomatoes, thinly sliced

In a small bowl, combine the vinegar, olive oil, mustard, salt and pepper. Whisk well. Place some basil on each slice of bread. Place a slice of bocconcini on top, add a little more basil, and fan 3 slices of cherry tomato on top. Drizzle a little vinaigrette on each one.

Oregano, Avocado and Roasted Red Pepper

1 sweet red pepper, cored and cut in half lengthwise
1 tsp. (5 mL) olive oil
Salt and freshly ground black pepper, to taste
2 ripe avocados, pitted and finely chopped
1 Tbsp. (15 mL) finely chopped fresh oregano
1 tsp. (5 mL) lemon juice
8 slices high-quality, very fresh, whole wheat bread
1 small head radicchio, washed and separated
8 sprigs oregano or parsley

Rub the pepper with olive oil, salt and pepper. Place cut side down on a cookie sheet and broil until the skin blackens and blisters. Remove from the oven and place directly into a plastic bag and twist the top closed. After 10 minutes, remove the pepper and peel the skin off. Cut each half into 4 thin strips and set aside. Mix the avocado with the oregano, lemon juice, salt and pepper.

Cut out the center of each slice of bread with a round, plain or fluted biscuit cutter. Place a piece of radicchio on each bread round.

Spoon approximately 1 Tbsp. (15 mL) of avocado on top, and place a slice of red pepper over it. Top with a small sprig of oregano or parsley.

Mint Shortbread with Chocolate Drizzle

A luxurious little nibble.

Makes approximately 20 cookies

¼ cup (60 mL) icing sugar
½ cup (120 mL) plus 1 Tbsp. (15 mL) butter
1½ cups (360 mL) unbleached all purpose flour
2 Tbsp. (30 mL) finely chopped fresh mint
2 oz. (57 g) dark semi-sweet chocolate, melted

Preheat the oven to 350°F (175°C).

Combine the icing sugar and butter and mix well. Stir in the flour and mint. Knead the dough gently a few times on a lightly floured surface. Chill for approximately 15 minutes to firm the dough a little.

Roll the dough out to approximately ¼ inch (.6 cm) thickness. Cut the cookies out with any shape cookie cutter you wish. Bake on an ungreased cookie sheet for 6–8 minutes, until the cookies are a pale golden color. Drizzle the melted chocolate on top with a fork, and cool on racks.

Serve on a bed of mint with a light sprinkling of icing sugar. Store any leftovers in an airtight container.

Lemon Thyme, Rose Petal, and Lavender Glazed Tea Cake

This pound cake is dressed for a tea party.

Makes approximately 10 slices

> 3 Tbsp. (45 mL) buttermilk
> 3 large eggs
> 1½ tsp. (7.5 mL) vanilla extract
> 1½ cups (360 mL) sifted cake flour
> ¾ cup (180 mL) sugar
> ¾ tsp. (4 mL) baking powder
> ¼ tsp. (1.2 mL) salt
> 1 Tbsp. (15 mL) lemon zest, finely chopped
> 2 Tbsp. (30 mL) fresh lemon thyme, finely chopped
> ¾ cup (180 mL) plus 1 Tbsp. (15 mL) unsalted butter at
>   room temperature
> 6 Tbsp. (90 mL) sugar
> ¼ cup (60 mL) fresh lemon juice
> 1 Tbsp. (30 mL) fresh lavender flowers, crushed
> ½ cup (120 mL) unsprayed edible rose petals

Preheat the oven to 350°F (175°C). Grease and flour an 8 × 4 inch (20 × 10 cm) loaf pan or a 9- to 10-inch (23- to 25-cm) round cake pan. (Measurements may vary slightly.)

Combine the buttermilk, eggs and vanilla in a medium bowl. Combine the cake flour, ¾ cup (180 mL) sugar, baking powder and salt in a large mixing bowl. Add the lemon zest and lemon thyme. Using an electric mixer on low speed, or by hand, beat the dry mixture for a few seconds to blend. Add the butter and half the egg mixture. Mix on low speed until the dry ingredients are moistened. Turn the speed up to medium and beat for 1 minute. Scrape the sides of the bowl down and add the remaining egg mixture in 2 batches, beating for 20 seconds after each addition.

Spoon the batter into the prepared cake pan and smooth the surface with a spatula. Bake for approximately 35–45 minutes in a round pan, 10–15 minutes longer in a loaf pan. The cake is done when a toothpick or knife inserted in it comes out clean. Cover the cake loosely with some buttered foil or parchment paper to prevent over-browning after it has been in the oven for 30 minutes.

Shortly before the cake is done, prepare the glaze. Combine the remaining sugar, lemon juice and lavender flowers in a small saucepan over medium heat, stirring until the sugar has dissolved completely, approximately 5 minutes.

As soon as the cake comes out of the oven, place the pan on a rack to cool. Poke the cake all over with a skewer and brush with half the glaze. Cool for 10 minutes. Loosen the sides of the cake with a spatula and invert it onto a lightly greased cooling rack. Poke the bottom of the cake with the skewer, brush with glaze and flip the cake back over onto the rack. Brush with the remaining glaze and allow the cake to cool completely. Serve at room temperature with a sprinkling of rose petals on top. This cake will keep for up to a week in the refrigerator, or 2–3 days at room temperature.

Lemon Verbena Iced Tea

The ultimate lemon-lover's tea.

Makes 6 cups (1.5 L)

12 sprigs lemon verbena, plus some for garnish
1 Earl Grey tea bag
6 cups (1.5 L) boiling water
2 trays ice cubes

Steep the verbena and the tea bag in boiling water until cooled. Add the ice and serve with a few extra sprigs of lemon verbena. If you prefer the tea sweet, add some sugar to the tea while it is hot.

Dungeness Crab Feast

There are two kinds of people: those who eat their crabmeat as they crack it, and those who patiently create an enviable pile, then eat it while the rest of the guests look on with slightly resentful looks on their faces. This is a simple but tantalizing menu that is wonderful with crisp white wine or champagne.

Boiled Fresh Dungeness Crab

Lemon Herb Butter

Noël's Retro Cocktail Sauce

Homemade Tartar Sauce

Creamy Curry Sauce

Wild Mixed Greens with Balsamic Maple Vinaigrette

Pavlova

Boiled Fresh Dungeness Crab

If you are uncomfortable cooking live crabs, ask your seafood store to prepare them for you on the day of your feast. Allow 1 crab per person.

Bring a large pot of water to a boil. Add a couple of bay leaves, a bouquet garni (a mixture of herbs tied together), some peppercorns and a few slices of lemon.

Place the crabs in the water so they are completely immersed. Boil for approximately 20 minutes. When the crabs turn bright red they are ready to eat. Remove them from the water and immerse them in cool water.

When the crabs are cool enough to handle, pull off the main shell of each one and clean out the guts. Crack the legs and claws on each crab with a mallet or hammer. Place a set of legs on each plate and put the crab shell back on top. Give each guest a finger bowl and provide a couple of larger bowls for discarding the shells. Place several nut-crackers around the table for sharing, and put out plenty of napkins.

Serve the crab with an assortment of sauces and crusty baguettes. If you feel ambitious, make your own. If you buy baguettes, warm them just before serving.

Lemon Herb Butter

This is the simplest way to dress crab.

Makes 1 cup (240 mL)

> ½ lb. (225 g) butter
> Juice of 1 lemon
> 1 cup (240 mL) mixed, finely chopped herbs (such as parsley, tarragon, basil and chives)

Combine all the ingredients in a saucepan and melt the butter. Do not boil. Serve the butter in 2 separate bowls.

Noël's Retro Cocktail Sauce

Noël has been making this for 40 years, with a few adjustments along the way.

Makes approximately 1¾ cups (420 mL)

> ¼ cup (60 mL) tomato ketchup
> 2 tsp. (10 mL) freshly grated horseradish root, or store-bought horseradish
> 1 tsp. (5 mL) lemon juice
> 1 ½ cups (360 mL) homemade (see below) or store-bought mayonnaise
> 2 Tbsp. (30 mL) red seafood cocktail sauce
> 2 Tbsp. (30 mL) finely chopped chives
> Hot pepper sauce, to taste
> Salt and freshly ground black pepper, to taste

Combine all the ingredients and taste for seasoning. Serve the sauce in 2 separate bowls.

Basic Mayonnaise

Mayonnaise is called for in three of the crab dips. If you prefer home-made, this recipe is simple and delicious.

Makes about 1½ cups (360 mL)

> 1 egg yolk
> 1 tsp. (5 mL) mustard
> ½ tsp. (2.5 mL) salt
> 1 tsp. (5 mL) lemon zest, finely chopped
> 2 tsp. (10 mL) fresh lemon juice
> 1 cup (240 mL) extra virgin olive oil

Combine the egg yolk, mustard, salt, zest and lemon juice in a food processor. Process until well blended. With the motor running, slowly drizzle in the olive oil and blend until thickened.

Homemade Tartar Sauce

It's well worth making your own tartar sauce.

Makes approximately 1½ cups (360 mL)

> 1 large dill pickle, finely chopped
> 2 shallots, finely chopped
> 2 Tbsp. (30 mL) capers
> 1 clove garlic, pressed
> 2 Tbsp. (30 mL) finely chopped fresh dill
> ½ tsp. (2.5 mL) lemon juice
> 1 ½ cups (360 mL) homemade (see page 122) or store-bought mayonnaise
> Salt and freshly ground black pepper, to taste

Combine all the ingredients, and taste for seasoning. Serve the sauce in 2 separate bowls.

Creamy Curry Sauce

This sauce is also great for dipping steamed artichokes.

Makes approximately 1½ cups (360 mL)

> 1 tsp. (5 mL) Madras curry powder
> ½ tsp. (2.5 mL) cumin powder
> ¼ tsp. (1.2 mL) cayenne pepper
> 1 ½ cups (360 mL) homemade (see page 122) or store-bought mayonnaise
> 1 tsp. (5 mL) lemon or lime juice
> 1 Tbsp. (15 mL) fresh tarragon, finely chopped
> Salt and freshly ground black pepper, to taste

In a small frying pan, combine the curry powder, cumin and cayenne. Toast lightly over low heat for 1 minute. Combine with all the other ingredients and taste for seasoning. Serve the sauce in 2 separate bowls.

Wild Mixed Greens with Balsamic Maple Vinaigrette

This recipe is Andrew's invention. The maple syrup adds a touch of sweetness to the sharp-tasting greens.

Serves 8

> 8 cups (2 L) mixed greens, such as red leaf lettuce, arugula,
>   radicchio, watercress, Belgian endive or spinach
> ¼ cup (60 mL) balsamic vinegar
> ¾ cup (175 mL) extra virgin olive oil
> 2 shallots, finely chopped
> 2 tsp. (10 mL) maple syrup
> 2 Tbsp. (30 mL) finely chopped chives
> Salt and freshly ground pepper, to taste
> 1 Tbsp. (15 mL) Dijon mustard

Wash the greens and place them in a salad bowl. Combine the remaining vinaigrette ingredients in a jar with a sealed lid and shake vigorously. Taste for seasoning and drizzle over the greens.

Pavlova

This recipe is adapted from the excellent *David Wood Food Book*. This is truly one of the great summer desserts. If you prefer not to make your own meringue, many bakeries sell individual nests, which you can fill with fruit and whipped cream.

Serves 6–8

> 4 egg whites, at room temperature
> ¼ tsp. (1.2 mL) salt
> ¼ tsp. (1.2 mL) cream of tartar
> ¾ cup plus 3 Tbsp. (225 mL) granulated sugar
> 1 Tbsp. (15 mL) cornstarch
> 1 tsp. (5 mL) white wine vinegar
> ½ tsp. (2.5 mL) pure vanilla extract
> 1½ cups (360 mL) whipping cream
> 2 Tbsp. (30 mL) finely chopped lemon balm

½ tsp. (2.5 mL) cinnamon (optional)

3 cups (720 mL), more or less, fresh fruit, such as kiwi, strawberries, raspberries, passion fruit, mango, papaya, pineapple or blueberries and blackberries

Preheat the oven to 275°F (135°C).

Line a large cookie sheet with parchment and trace a circle approximately 9 inches (23 cm) in diameter in the center, using a plate or bowl as a guide. Remove the parchment and lightly grease the cookie sheet. Reverse the parchment and smooth it onto the cookie sheet. You will be able to see the circle through the paper, but the ink or pencil lead won't be picked up by the meringue.

Beat the egg whites with the salt and cream of tartar until they hold a stiff peak. Add the sugar 2 Tbsp. (30 mL) at a time, beating well between additions. The meringue should be thick and glossy. Gently beat in the cornstarch, vinegar and vanilla. With a large spoon, scoop the meringue onto the parchment paper. Using the circle as a guide, create a large mound with a high dome in the center. Bake for 1 ½–2 hours, until pale golden and crisp on the outside. It should be soft in the middle. If the meringue becomes overly brown after the first hour of baking, turn the oven down to 225°F (105°C).

Remove the pan from the oven and allow the meringue to cool completely on a rack. The meringue may collapse in the center as it cools; this doesn't present a problem.

Combine the whipping cream, lemon balm and cinnamon, if desired, and whip to soft peaks. Place the meringue on a serving platter. With a sharp knife, remove the top of the dome and fill the crater of the meringue volcano with about half the fruit. Spread the whipped cream on the top and all over the outside of the meringue. Arrange the rest of the fruit attractively on the whipped cream. Replace the dome on top of the fruit. Scatter some extra lemon balm sprigs and edible flowers randomly over the top. Refrigerate until ready to serve.

French Picnic

In the south of France there are predominant flavors—garlic, basil, olives and anchovies—that are used to create many savory dishes. This menu evokes the ambience of that region. Choose a location with a wonderful view, spread out a large picnic blanket, and don't forget the wine.

Goat Cheese Tart with Fresh Thyme and Caramelized Shallots

Black Olive and Basil Tapenade

French Bread with Fresh Sage and Rosemary

Tomatoes with Eggplant Caviar Provençal

Hard-boiled Eggs with Garlic and Tarragon

Fresh Poached Local Prawns with Aïoli

Dandelion Greens (Pissenlit) with a Chervil and Shallot Vinaigrette

Seasonal Fruit in Eau de Vie

Goat Cheese Tart with Fresh Thyme and Caramelized Shallots

You can use good-quality cow's or ewe's milk cream cheese instead of goat cheese if you prefer.

Serves 8

>   Pastry for a 12-inch (30-cm) tart
>   1 Tbsp. (15 mL) butter
>   1 Tbsp. (15 mL) olive oil
>   8 shallots, thinly sliced
>   ½ cup (120 mL) white wine or dry white vermouth
>   8 oz. (225 g) creamy goat cheese
>   ½ cup (120 mL) fresh chives, chopped
>   2 Tbsp. (30 mL) finely chopped fresh thyme
>   Salt and freshly ground black pepper, to taste
>   3 large free-range eggs

Use the pastry recipe from the Rhubarb Tart with Sweet Cicely and Toasted Almond Cream (page 53), leaving out the sugar, or choose one of your own favorites. Prepare the pastry and prebake according to the tart recipe.

Melt the butter and olive oil over medium heat. Add the shallots and sauté over medium-low heat for 10 minutes. Add the wine or vermouth and cook for another 10 minutes, or until caramelized. Set aside.

Preheat the oven to 375°F (190°C).

Process the cheese, chives, thyme, salt and pepper in a food processor until smooth. With the motor running, add 1 egg at a time, blending well. Distribute the shallots evenly in the pie crust. Spread the cheese mixture on top. Bake for 20–30 minutes, until the top is golden and the filling has set. Allow to cool for 15 minutes before serving.

Black Olive and Basil Tapenade

This tapenade should keep for a month in the refrigerator. It is also excellent tossed with pasta.

Makes approximately 1½ cups (360 mL)

> 1 cup pitted black olives, such as kalamata, Sicilian, niçoise, or Moroccan
> 2–3 cloves garlic
> 1¾-oz. (50-g) can anchovies, drained and rinsed
> ¼ cup (60 mL) chopped fresh basil
> ½ cup (120 mL) olive oil

Process the olives, garlic, anchovies and basil in a food processor until smooth. With the machine running, slowly add the oil. Serve with crisp toast or melba toast rounds.

French Bread with Fresh Sage and Rosemary

You can make your own bread, or buy a good-quality French bread.

> 1 loaf French bread
> 1 egg, beaten
> ¼ cup (60 mL) chopped fresh sage and rosemary

Preheat the oven to 300°F (150°C).

Combine the egg with the herbs. Lightly brush the mixture on the bread. Place in the oven for 15 minutes, until the glaze is sealed and cooked.

Tomatoes with Eggplant Caviar Provençal

An exquisite fresh accompaniment to any menu. The word "caviar" describes the luxurious appearance of the eggplant. Serve leftover eggplant as a spread with bread or crackers.

Serves 6

> 3 eggplants, approximately 1 lb. (455 g) each
> 2 Tbsp. (30 mL) olive oil
> 3 cloves garlic, finely chopped or pressed
> 2 shallots, finely chopped
> 1 Tbsp. (15 mL) finely chopped basil
> ⅓ cup (80 mL) olive oil
> Juice of 1 lemon
> Salt and freshly ground black pepper, to taste
> 6 Roma tomatoes, sliced in half widthwise
> 1 Tbsp. (15 mL) finely chopped parsley

Preheat the oven to 350°F (175°C).

Slice the eggplants in half lengthwise. Spread the 2 Tbsp. (30 mL) olive oil on a cookie sheet and place the eggplant cut side down on it. Bake for approximately 45 minutes, until the flesh is very soft. Remove the seed strips and scoop out the flesh, discarding the skin.

Place in a food processor and add the garlic, shallots and basil. With the motor running, slowly add the remaining olive oil, lemon juice, salt and pepper.

Slice a small amount off the bottom of each tomato half, so the tomato will sit flat. Scoop 1 tsp. (5 mL) of flesh out of each tomato. Fill the tomato with the eggplant mixture and sprinkle with chopped parsley.

Hard-boiled Eggs with Garlic and Tarragon

At Ravenhill we collect our own free-range eggs from "the girls."

Makes 12

> 6 free-range eggs, carefully scrubbed
> 10 cloves garlic, peeled
> 3 anchovy fillets
> 1 Tbsp. (15 mL) capers
> 2 Tbsp. (30 mL) finely chopped fresh tarragon
> 3 Tbsp. (45 mL) extra virgin olive oil
> ½ tsp. (2.5 mL) red wine vinegar
> Salt and freshly ground black pepper, to taste
> 1 Tbsp. (15 mL) finely chopped fresh parsley
> 1 tsp. (5 mL) cayenne, black pepper or paprika
> 12 small sprigs of watercress

Place the eggs and garlic cloves in a saucepan of cold water. Bring to a boil, and simmer for 10 minutes over medium heat. Cool the eggs and garlic in cold water. Peel the eggs and cut them in half lengthwise.

Place the garlic, anchovies, capers, tarragon and egg yolks in a mortar or mixing bowl. Pound with a pestle or a wooden spoon until the mixture is pastelike. Slowly beat in the olive oil. Add the vinegar, salt, pepper and parsley.

Fill the egg white halves with the mixture, sprinkle with cayenne, pepper or paprika and place a sprig of watercress on each. Chill and serve.

Fresh Poached Local Prawns
with Aïoli

Made with freshly harvested garlic, the aïoli is a vivid companion to the prawns.

Serves 4–6

  2 cups (475 mL) water
  1 cup (240 mL) white wine or dry white
     vermouth
  1 bay leaf
  1 tsp. (5 mL) whole peppercorns
  Zest and juice of ½ lemon
  18–20 medium-size fresh prawns
  1 Tbsp. (15 mL) finely chopped fennel frond
  1 recipe Basil Aïoli (page 132)

Combine the water, wine or vermouth, bay leaf, peppercorns and lemon zest in a deep large frying pan. Bring to a simmer and add the prawns. Simmer gently for 2–3 minutes, stirring occasionally, until the prawns have turned pink. Strain and cool.

Peel the prawns, leaving the tail on. Squeeze the lemon juice over top and sprinkle with the fennel. Serve with a bowl of Basil Aïoli.

Dill

For some unknown reason dill can be difficult to grow. At Ravenhill our best dill seems to come from plants that have self-seeded the previous fall, especially if they have accidentally grown under a plastic tunnel reserved for basil. They are obviously good companion plants!

I noticed this year that the cover prevented the normal aphid infestation on the dill. Next year I shall scatter some seed in October and try growing the May and June sowings under a floating row cover.

Basil Aïoli

A blast of basil in an already pungent sauce. It marries well with the prawns and can also be served as a condiment with the Barbecued Flank Steak Marinated with Basil and Garlic (page 108).

Serves 6

> 8–10 cloves garlic, peeled
> 1 cup (240 mL) firmly packed fresh basil
> 2 egg yolks, room temperature
> Salt and freshly ground black pepper
> Juice of 1 lemon
> 1 tsp. (5 mL) Dijon mustard
> 1½ cups (360 mL) extra virgin olive oil

Purée the garlic and basil in a food processor. Whisk the egg yolks in a small bowl until light and smooth. Add the yolks, salt, pepper, lemon juice and mustard to the food processor and process until smooth. Add the oil slowly while the machine is running. Continue processing until the mixture is thick, shiny and firm. Refrigerate until ready to use.

Dandelion Greens (Pissenlit) with a Chervil and Shallot Vinaigrette

You can pick your own greens in the country when the leaves are young and tender, or sow your own. Noël found a package of seeds in France, called Pissenlit, and brought them home, thinking they were some exotic green. She later discovered that the direct translation of Pissenlit is "wet the bed," as dandelion greens are a natural diuretic.

Serves 4

40 young dandelion leaves
⅓ cup (80 mL) extra virgin olive oil
2 Tbsp. (30 mL) red wine vinegar
2 cloves garlic, peeled and pressed
1 Tbsp. (15 mL) fresh chervil leaves
2 shallots, finely chopped
1 tsp. (5 mL) Dijon mustard
Salt and freshly ground black pepper, to taste
2 slices stale bread

Wash and dry the dandelion leaves. Wrap them in a towel and refrigerate for at least 20 minutes, until they are cold and crisp.

In a small bowl, whisk together the olive oil, vinegar, garlic, chervil, shallots, mustard, salt and pepper.

Cut the bread into large croutons and lightly toast for approximately 2–3 minutes under the broiler.

Place the dandelion leaves in a bowl, top with the croutons, pour the dressing on top, and toss.

Seasonal Fruit in Eau de Vie

Eau de vie is traditionally created by distilling a powerful alcoholic liquid from grape skins, seeds and stems left over from wine-making, and is also called grappa. You can also use good-quality vodka or unflavored schnapps to preserve fruit, as I have done in this recipe.

Pick raspberries in season, allow them to macerate for 4–6 weeks, and serve them at a picnic in August. In August, preserve blackberries, which will be ready to eat in early to mid-September. In the late summer and early fall try the fig, plum and peach combination, and enjoy it in early October.

To serve, cut large fruits into bite-size pieces and serve with a few large spoonfuls of fruity liquid. It is wonderful with ice cream or cake. Consume the contents of each jar within a year.

Raspberries in Eau de Vie

1 lb. (455 g) raspberries
1 cup (240 mL) sugar
2 sprigs mint
2–3 raspberry leaves
2 cups (475 mL) vodka, grappa or plain schnapps

Layer the fruit, sugar, mint sprigs and raspberry leaves in a large sterilized jar. Pour the alcohol over the fruit. Seal the jar and set in a cool, dark place for 4–6 weeks. During this time, occasionally turn the jar upside down (and right side up again) to redistribute the alcohol and the natural fruit sugars.

Figs, Plums and Peaches in Eau de Vie

  ½ lb. (225 g) fresh figs, rinsed and dried
  ½ lb. (225 g) fresh plums, rinsed, dried and pitted
  ½ lb. (225 g) fresh peaches, rinsed, dried, halved and pitted
  2–3 sprigs lemon verbena
  1½ cups (360 mL) sugar
  4–6 cups (950 mL–1.5 L) vodka, grappa or plain schnapps

Use the method outlined on page 134.

September
and
October

Harvest Heaven

Garlic is the catsup of intellectuals.

—ANONYMOUS

You've buttered your bread, now sleep in it.

—GRACIE ALLEN

*Show me another pleasure like dinner, which comes every day
and lasts an hour.*

—TALLEYRAND

*And I never went to work without a sprig of basil in my
cleavage. Men like a woman who smells of good food.*

—EIGHTY-SIX-YEAR-OLD
ROSE PISTOLA

IN OUR AREA OF THE PENINSULA, fall is a mixture of endings and beginnings. We always attend the annual fall fair organized by the North and South Saanich Agricultural Society, which has been running since 1868 and claims to be the oldest agricultural fair in western Canada. My great-uncle George Bradley-Dyne was president of the fair in 1900. He and my great-aunt Katie Bradley-Dyne were well known for breeding excellent cows and horses. I love visiting the magnificent cows, horses, pigs, ducks and other poultry in the animal barns at the fair. The young donkeys, miniature horses and baby pigs touch my heart. I admire the people who preserve the old breeds out of a passion for retaining our agricultural history.

The domestic arts section also contains samples of almost-lost arts. Jams and jellies glow ruby-red and amber. Patchwork quilts hanging from the ceiling demonstrate the patience and skill of needle-women who are still creating the way their ancestors did in the 19th century.

The competition in the vegetable-growing section is fierce. Short notes are left explaining why certain runner beans or onions did not win. Every vegetable has to be set out according to the rule book, and no deviations are permitted. There are beets and squashes as large as a giant's head, and perfect apples that look like identical quintuplets—no scabs or variations. Dahlias in glowing colors set the hall alive with their brilliance. The varied and intriguing flower arrangements show how intense the competition is. In our first few years on the farm Andrew and I entered our vegetables and herbs and came home with ribbons which we proudly hung in the kitchen. As we became more skilled at the herb business, we stopped entering, but we still go and look and think, like many people, "My vegetables are as good, or better, than those."

The fair draws thousands of people and the fields are plugged with cars. City kids stare goggle-eyed at the number of animals, and delight in the sheep-herding and the dizzying, throat-wrenching carnival rides. We can hear the noise of the fair at the farm, enticing us to the fairgrounds to enjoy the end of summer.

Such events create a great feeling of community and give us a sense of place, so important for a stable, productive life. The fair is proof of the pleasure of activities such as gardening, sewing and caring for animals—real activities that link us to the earth. I think we all have a deep psychological need to know where we come from. This does not mean we should not travel or move to other places, but having a sense of place and roots helps us create new lives as adults.

The end of the summer brings the last herb Sunday of the season at Ravenhill. We hold an art show in the barn. One level is filled with beautiful golden landscapes by Yumi Kono, a Japanese Canadian artist. The upper level is filled with sculptures by her friend Will Gordon, amazing constructions made out of things he finds in nature. Driftwood, bones and twigs all find their way into Will's sculptures. The peacocks and hens wander through the pieces, adding new meaning to the barn art.

In September and October produce starts to stack up in the kitchen and I get a case of preserving anxiety. We need fewer things now for the cupboards because the children have long since left, our appetites have become smaller, and we have dietary restrictions. We still make blackberry jam and argue whether the seeds should be left in or not. I make mint jelly to serve with our lamb. I also make rosemary and tarragon jelly, both of which are good with pork and chicken. We freeze some peas, although on the whole my taste for frozen vegetables has gone. In this climate we can usually eat out of the garden all winter with a little help from cold frames and kind weather. One year, though, we had a terrible freeze and lost all our winter vegetables in January. Gone were the kale, greens and carrots. I felt I had lost my grocery store.

I have more time for myself in September and October. I clean the goose pond, to the delight of the geese who go berserk with joyful splashing after I leave. The second hatch of baby swallows leaves the barn. I will miss their cheeping and the swoops of their parents constantly feeding them. This year the fig tree produced well. A fresh fig for break- fast on an old Chinese plate is an amazing experience.

The last flurry of guests comes before it is time for everyone to return to work and their regular lives. Cousins, sister, brother, nieces and nephews all gather on Saturna Island, where the present owners of my grandfather's house have invited us to stay for the weekend. We sleep in the rooms in which our mothers were born and raised, trying to imagine what their lives were like in this house before 1920. We sit talking on the verandah, eyeing the fifth-generation children for family likenesses.

In 1886 my 16-year-old grandfather arrived on Saturna from England and created a life and family. He found my Irish grandmother in San Francisco after he became ill during the Yukon gold rush. The doctors did not give him much hope for his ailing lungs and advised him to go to San Francisco, where my grandmother was his nurse. Romance bloomed and they returned to Saturna Island. It must have been a cultural shock when she found herself on such an isolated island. She was famed for her cooking, gardening skills and wicked Irish temper, qualities which have been inherited in varying degrees by her descendants.

The menus and recipes for September and October make rich use of the fall harvest. I first made vegetarian chili in a baked pumpkin shell years ago, after learning how to successfully bake the shell from Marion Morash's *Victory Garden Cookbook*. This is one of the best vegetable cookbooks I have come across. She gives infinite variations on each vegetable. Morash runs a restaurant and did the cooking section of the "Victory Garden" television show.

Andrew grows a large French pumpkin, 'Rouge Vif d'Etampes,' which has a beautiful red-orange color and tastes delicious. I decorate the kitchen with these pumpkins all winter, and they provide lovely hits of color in the winter gloom. In American seed catalogues, 'Rouge Vif d'Etampes' can sometimes be found under the name 'Cinderella'.

The green tomato pie has a Mennonite heritage; a friend brought it for dessert one year and I loved it. It is tangy with lemon zest and cinnamon, and should be served with whipped cream or sweetened, good-quality yogurt. This meal needs lots of pickles to sharpen the flavors of the beans and cabbage, and we have included yellow pickled beans and cucumbers.

The dinner rolls are based on my favorite, versatile French bread recipe which also appears in my second cookbook, *Winter Pleasures*. In *Herbal Celebrations* it also serves as a base for the pizza crust in July and August's Basil and Garlic Dinner menu. This recipe evolved after years of baking. Even beginners have had success with it—I have had long-distance telephone calls from people thanking me for the recipe and their first baking success.

The Thanksgiving Dinner menu has a few variations on the norm. Instead of the ubiquitous turkey, we have chosen goose. Young geese are available frozen in most supermarkets. I cooked a goose once for a Christmas dinner class. As the students arrived my fat geese honked at them. The class was very relieved to hear it wasn't one of these geese that was to be the entrée. We have always kept geese. We love watching the goslings, but have never eaten them. This may be culinary cowardice, but it is easier to buy a prepared goose, all neat and tidy from the supermarket. I think if I was left on my own I would become vegetarian.

The method of cooking your goose, which I found after some research in Julia Child's compendium *How To Cook*, is simple and gets rid of the goose fat. The trick is to steam it first and then roast it, which produces a very moist, tender bird. Julia Child is a mentor to many cooks, professional and otherwise. I once stood beside her at a buffet dinner at a large cooking conference. It was a delight to watch her quickly slurp down raw oysters with great pleasure. Encouraged, I joined in with relish.

Our sage cornbread stuffing with spicy Italian sausage is tastier than old-fashioned stuffing with tired, dried sage and poultry seasoning. This stuffing has flavor and zap. The pumpkin and red cabbage go well with rich goose meat, and a rich, creamy potato celeriac purée makes a change from mashed potatoes. Dessert is pumpkin pie made chiffon-fashion, a much lighter version than plain pumpkin pie. I first made this from *The Joy of Cooking* when I was about 18 and my version of this pie has been a favorite ever since.

For our fall celebrations, I love to make centerpieces of apples, squashes and vegetables. I twist strands of ivy around the candelabra and the tallest person lights the candles before dinner. I ask someone to create a good grace to begin the family dinner, for we should be very thankful for good food, the harvest, good friends and family. We send these good wishes out into the crisp fall evening and enjoy.

It is getting darker earlier. We take walks in the crisper weather now that we have more time. I collect apples in baskets, making applesauce for my new granddaughter. This child has had organic food from the beginning and is the picture of rosy good health. The woodpile in the old basement is stacked and our evening fires are cheering and warming. When we are alone we pull up to the fire and have our dinner there, leaving the dining table in the dark. When company comes I clear off all the papers, mail and ongoing projects, and we eat at the dining room table. The golden fall days will soon change to gray, rainy November and the dark nights of a coastal winter, when we will really need good cooking to get us through.

Vegetarian Fall Splendor

In the fall there are many beautiful squashes and pumpkins in the garden and at the local markets. We decorate the kitchen with them and put a display on the patio table. This heartwarming harvest supper features chili encased in a large orange pumpkin. Using vegetables as receptacles for other food has a long history, and is both efficient and attractive.

Pumpkin Black Bean Chili with Cilantro and Crème Fraîche

Wild Rice Pilaf with Apples and Roasted Pine Nuts

Rosemary and Caraway Cheese Rolls

Pickled Cucumbers or Yellow Beans

*Savoy Cabbage Coleslaw with Grilled Peppers
and Sweet Marjoram*

Green Tomato Tart

Pumpkin Black Bean Chili with Cilantro and Crème Fraîche

The chili tastes richer when it's made a few hours or a day ahead. Put the chili in the baked pumpkin just before serving. If desired, add cooked chicken to this dish.

Serves 10–12

- 1 large pumpkin
- 3 Tbsp. (45 mL) butter, melted
- ¼ cup (60 mL) olive oil
- 2 medium red onions, finely chopped
- 1 bulb garlic, finely chopped
- 6 shallots, finely chopped
- 1 Tbsp. (15 mL) cumin, lightly toasted
- 1 Tbsp. (15 mL) chili powder, or less, to taste
- 1 Tbsp. (15 mL) fennel seeds
- Salt and freshly ground black pepper, to taste
- 1 green bell pepper, finely chopped
- 1 lb. (455 g) mushrooms, finely chopped
- 1 cup (240 mL) robust red wine
- 1 lb. (455 g) black beans, soaked, cooked and rinsed, or 3 14-oz. (398-mL) cans black beans
- 1 28-oz. (796-mL) can whole tomatoes, puréed or chopped
- 1 lb. (455 g) fresh tomatoes, chopped
- 1 8-oz. (227-mL) can tomato paste
- 1 bunch cilantro, finely chopped
- 1 cup (240 mL) finely chopped mixed fresh herbs, such as oregano and basil
- Juice and zest of 1 lime
- Hot pepper sauce, to taste
- 1 cup (240 mL) fresh parsley, a mix of curly and flat Italian, finely chopped

Preheat the oven to 375°F (190°C).

Carefully slice a lid off the top of the pumpkin. Clean out the seeds and membranes, leaving the flesh. Reserve the seeds to roast as a snack. Brush the melted butter inside the pumpkin. Replace the lid on the pumpkin and bake for approximately 40–45 minutes, depending on the size. Be careful not to overcook the pumpkin or it will collapse. Keep the pumpkin at room temperature after baking.

While the pumpkin is baking, heat the olive oil in a large heavy pot over medium heat and sauté the onions, garlic and shallots for approximately 5 minutes. Add the cumin, chili powder, fennel seeds, salt and pepper. Sauté for a few more minutes. Add the green pepper and mushrooms, and cook for approximately 5 minutes more. Add the red wine, bring back to a simmer and stir in the black beans. Add the canned and fresh tomatoes and tomato paste and simmer for approximately 30 minutes. Add the cilantro and mixed fresh herbs. Taste for seasoning and add the lime juice, zest and as much hot pepper sauce as desired.

Ladle the chili into the baked pumpkin shell. When you ladle out the chili, scoop some pumpkin flesh away from the sides and serve the pumpkin and chili together. Place hot pepper sauce on the table for daring diners. Serve with a large bowl of crème fraîche and a bowl of freshly chopped parsley to sprinkle on top.

Crème Fraîche

A creamy, sour delight you can use in many soups and sauces.

Makes approximately 3 cups (720 mL)

    2 cups (475 mL) whipping cream
    3 Tbsp. (45 mL) sour cream
    1 cup (240 mL) buttermilk

In a glass or a non-reactive bowl, whisk together all the ingredients. Cover with cheesecloth or a tea towel and leave at room temperature overnight. Refrigerate for 4 hours before using. Use within 2 weeks.

Wild Rice Pilaf with Apples and Roasted Pine Nuts

Nutty and fruity, this dish would also be an excellent accompaniment for game, fowl or pork.

Serves 6–8

> 3 cups (720 mL) water
> 1 cup (240 mL) wild rice
> 1 bay leaf
> 2 cups (475 mL) vegetable or chicken stock
> 1 cup (240 mL) brown rice
> ¼ cup (60 mL) extra virgin olive oil
> 1 tsp. (5 mL) lemon thyme or English thyme leaves
> Zest and juice of 1 orange
> 2 tart apples, such as Granny Smith, peeled, cored, sliced and
>   reserved in water
> 2 Tbsp. (30 mL) chopped fresh Italian flat-leaf parsley
> ½ cup (120 mL) roasted pine nuts
> Salt and freshly ground black pepper, to taste

Preheat the oven to 350°F (175°C).

Bring the water to a boil in a medium saucepan. Add the wild rice and bay leaf. Cover and simmer for approximately 35–40 minutes, until the rice is just tender. Drain off any excess water and transfer the rice to a large bowl.

Bring the stock and brown rice to a boil in a heavy saucepan. Cover tightly and reduce the heat to low. Simmer until just tender, approximately 25–30 minutes. Add the brown rice to the wild rice.

Mix in the olive oil, thyme, orange juice and zest, and the apples. Place the rice mixture in an ovenproof casserole dish, cover with aluminum foil and bake for approximately 20 minutes, until the rice is soft and the pilaf is heated throughout. Mix in the parsley and pine nuts. Season to taste and serve hot.

Rosemary and Caraway Cheese Rolls

This recipe is a variation of Noël's basic French bread recipe. Oka cheese is a strong, smooth cheese made by monks in Quebec.

Makes 16 rolls

> ½ cup (120 mL) warm water
> 1 tsp. (5 mL) sugar
> ¼ tsp. (1.2 mL) ground ginger
> 2 Tbsp. (30 mL) dried yeast
> 5 cups (1.2 L) unbleached white flour
> 2 cups (475 mL) warm water
> 2 Tbsp. (30 mL) sugar
> 1½ tsp. (7.5 mL) salt
> 2 Tbsp. (30 mL) olive oil
> ½ cup (120 mL) oka cheese
> 1 Tbsp. (15 mL) chopped rosemary
> 1 tsp. (5 mL) caraway seeds
> 1 cup (240 mL) flour
> 1 egg beaten with 1 tsp. (5 mL) water

Preheat the oven to 400°F (200°C).

Combine the ½ cup (120 mL) warm water, 1 tsp. (5 mL) sugar, ginger and yeast in a bowl and let stand until bubbling well, about 10 minutes. (The addition of the ginger improves the yeast.)

Place 5 cups (1.2 L) flour in a large mixing bowl and make a well in the middle of the flour. Put the 2 cups (475 mL) warm water, the bubbling yeast mixture and the 2 Tbsp. (30 mL) sugar in the depression. Mix enough flour into the yeast mixture to slightly thicken it. Let stand for 20 minutes. The yeast mixture will mound up and bubble in the center.

Add the salt, oil, cheese, rosemary and caraway seeds and stir in the rest of the flour in the bowl. Mix well with a wooden spoon; the dough will be stiff.

Put the last cup (240 mL) of flour on a smooth surface and turn out the dough. Knead firmly and with energy for 10 minutes. Set the timer so you do not cheat. When done, the dough should form a smooth, non-sticky ball. Lightly oil the bowl and the dough and replace the dough in the bowl. Cover with a clean cloth and let rise for at least 2 hours, until doubled in size.

Punch down the dough and cut it into 16 pieces, each roughly half the size of a tennis ball. Form each piece into a ball and place them 1½ inches (3.8 cm) apart on a cookie sheet lightly sprinkled with cornmeal or flour. Cover with a tea towel and let proof for approximately 20 minutes.

Brush with the egg wash. Put a pan of water on the bottom rack of the preheated oven. Give each roll a quick, crisscross slash, and place the pan in the oven. Bake for approximately 20–30 minutes, until golden. Cool the rolls on a rack.

Corn Salad

This tender salad green can be grown in a cold frame and eaten for most of the winter. Sow seeds in August and September.

Pickled Cucumbers or Yellow Beans

At the end of the summer there is often such an abundance of vegetables that we can't keep up with them, and we turn to pickling to preserve some summer goodness for the rest of the year. I adapted this quick pickling technique from Alice Waters' book *Chez Panisse Vegetables*. You can use it to pickle many of your favorite firm vegetables, such as cauliflower or carrots. They will keep at least 1 month in the refrigerator.

Makes 4–5 cups (950 mL–1.2 L)

> ½ lb. (225 g) yellow wax beans, topped and tailed, or cucumbers, thinly sliced
> 3 cloves garlic, peeled and sliced in half
> 2 shallots, peeled and sliced in half
> ½ tsp. (2.5 mL) coriander seed
> 1 small hot chili, such as serrano
> ⅛ tsp. (.5 mL) whole black peppercorns
> 1 bay leaf
> 1 sprig of a favorite herb, such as basil, thyme, rosemary or tarragon
> 2 cups (475 mL) white wine vinegar or apple cider vinegar
> 1 cup (240 mL) dry white wine or dry white vermouth
> 1¼ cups (300 mL) water
> 1 Tbsp. (15 mL) kosher salt or good quality sea salt
> 2 Tbsp. (30 mL) sugar

Place the beans or cucumbers in a sterilized glass jar with a good seal. Add the garlic, shallots, coriander, chili, peppercorns, bay leaf and herb sprig.

Put the vinegar, wine or vermouth, water, salt and sugar in a saucepan, bring to a boil and boil for 1 minute. Remove from the heat, let cool slightly so the jar does not break and pour over the vegetables. Cover and cool completely at room temperature before refrigerating. The pickles will be ready in 48 hours, but will taste even better after a week.

Savoy Cabbage Coleslaw with Grilled Peppers and Sweet Marjoram

A refreshing change from traditional creamy coleslaw, this has the mild, yet distinct taste of sweet marjoram.

Serves 6–8

⅓ cup (60 mL) rice wine vinegar

⅔ cup (160 mL) olive oil

1 Tbsp. (15 mL) soy sauce

1 clove garlic, pressed

½ tsp. (2.5 mL) sesame oil

½ tsp. (2.5 mL) sambal oelek or hot sauce

1 red sweet pepper, cored and sliced in ½ inch (1.2 cm) rings

1 green sweet pepper, cored and sliced in ½ inch (1.2 cm) rings

1 savoy cabbage, thinly sliced

1 red onion, halved and thinly sliced

2 Tbsp. (30 mL) finely chopped fresh sweet marjoram

Salt and freshly ground black pepper, to taste

Whisk the vinegar, olive oil, soy sauce, garlic, sesame oil and sambal oelek together and set aside.

Heat a grill or barbecue to medium. Brush the peppers with a little vinaigrette and grill quickly, about 1 minute per side. Combine the cabbage, peppers, onion and marjoram in a glass bowl or on a platter. Toss with the vinaigrette. Season to taste.

Green Tomato Tart

Green tomatoes are delicious. Tart, yet sweet, they suit both desserts and savory dishes. (Try them pan-fried with eggs for breakfast.) Serve this tart with fresh whipped cream.

Serves 8

> Pastry for a single-crust pie
> 1⅓ cups (320 mL) brown sugar
> 2 Tbsp. (30 mL) cornmeal
> 3 Tbsp. (45 mL) flour
> ¼ tsp. (1.2 mL) salt
> ½ tsp. (2.5 mL) cinnamon
> ½ tsp. (2.5 mL) nutmeg
> 1 Tbsp. (15 mL) lemon thyme leaves
> 6 medium, firm, green tomatoes, thinly sliced
> Juice and zest of 1 lemon
> ¼ cup (60 mL) cold butter

Prepare and bake the pie crust. Use the recipe for Rhubarb Tart (page 53) or your own favorite recipe.

Combine the brown sugar, cornmeal, flour, salt, cinnamon, nutmeg and lemon thyme. Sprinkle 2 Tbsp. (30 mL) of the mixture on the cooked pastry shell. Layer the tomatoes around the tart shell in a circular fashion, so they overlap each other, until the tart bottom is completely covered. Sprinkle the lemon juice and zest over the tomatoes.

Blend the butter with the remaining sugar mixture using your fingers or a pastry blender, until it resembles coarse bread crumbs. Cover the top of the pie with the crumb mixture and bake at 350°F (175°C) for approximately 30 minutes, until golden brown and bubbly. Cool for 10 minutes before serving.

Thanksgiving Dinner

Thanksgiving is a marvelous time to feast with friends and give thanks for the harvest. Roast goose has less meat than a turkey, so you may want to cook more than one. We raise geese on the farm, but no one has the courage to butcher them, so they live to a ripe old age. Young frozen geese are available at large food markets or butchers, or you may find a farmer who raises geese by checking local newspapers.

Goat Cheese Gratin

Roast Goose with Sausage and Sage Cornbread Stuffing

Sicilian Sweet and Sour Pumpkin with Fresh Mint

Red Cabbage with Red Wine, Bay Leaves and Thyme

Potato Celeriac Purée

Spinach and Swiss Chard Bundles

Pumpkin Chiffon Pie

Goat Cheese Gratin

A cosy, comforting starter that goes well with a large glass of red wine.

Serves 4–6

> 10–12 oz. (285–340 g) soft goat cheese, cubed
> 2 tsp. (10 mL) finely chopped fresh rosemary
> 2 tsp. (10 mL) finely chopped fresh oregano
> 1½–2 cups (360–475 mL) tomato sauce
> 24 good-quality black pitted olives, such as Moroccan or niçoise
> 1 Tbsp. (15 mL) Italian flat-leaf parsley

Preheat the broiler.

Place the cheese on the bottom of a baking dish. Sprinkle with half the rosemary and oregano. Spoon over just enough tomato sauce to cover the cheese. Sprinkle with the olives and remaining herbs.

Place under the broiler until the cheese is melted and the tomato sauce is sizzling, about 2–3 minutes. Sprinkle with the parsley. Serve with breadsticks or your favorite crackers.

Roast Goose with Sausage and Sage Cornbread Stuffing

The dark, dense, rich goose meat is a pleasant change from turkey. The method for cooking the goose has been adapted from Julia Child. Steaming the goose before roasting it makes the meat moister and less fatty. Duck can also be cooked using this recipe.

Serves 8–10

To roast the goose:

> 1 9- to 11-lb. (4- to 5-kg) young goose
> Juice of 1 lemon
> Salt, to taste
> 1 recipe Sausage and Sage Cornbread Stuffing (page 156)

1 each, large carrot, onion and celery stalk, coarsely chopped
1 Tbsp. (15 mL) finely chopped fresh rosemary
2 cups (475 mL) red wine, white wine or water
½ cup (120 mL) port, blended with 1½ Tbsp. (22.5 mL) cornstarch

Rinse the goose and pat it dry. Remove any excess loose fat. Cut off the tips of the wings. Chop the neck and wing tips, combine with the heart and gizzard, and simmer for 2 hours in about 4 cups (950 mL) of water. Strain, degrease and refrigerate until you make the gravy. You should have about 2 cups (475 mL) of stock.

Place the goose in a roasting pan with a rack and a tight-fitting lid (or foil). Prick the skin in numerous places to help render the fat. Rub the goose inside and out with lemon juice, and lightly salt the inside of the cavity. Place approximately 2 inches (5 cm) of water in the bottom of the roasting pan. Cover tightly and steam on top of the stove for 45 minutes to an hour, periodically checking the water level.

Remove the steamed goose from the roasting pan and allow it to cool for 15–20 minutes. Pour the liquid out of the roaster; it will be mainly fat. You can save this for sautéing potatoes, or separate and discard the fat and reserve the liquid for cooking the goose.

Stuff the goose with the cornbread sausage stuffing, packing it in tightly. Place a double sheet of foil over the rack and lay the goose on it, breast side down. Strew the chopped vegetables and rosemary in the pan around the goose. Pour in half the wine or water and about 2 cups (240 mL) of the steaming liquid, adding more liquid and wine during cooking as needed. Cover tightly and braise for 1–1½ hours, depending on the size of the bird. Check it and baste it every 20 minutes.

Turn the goose breast side up and baste it with the pan juices. Leave the cover off if the skin needs browning, or keep the goose partially covered if it is already brown. Continue roasting for approximately 30 minutes more, basting once or twice. The drumstick should feel quite loose and tender when wiggled. The temperature in the center of the thickest part of the breast should be at least

185°F (85°C). Remove the goose to a carving board or platter, leaving the vegetables in the pan. Turn off the oven and place the goose in the oven to keep it warm. Degrease the roasting pan, and pour in the previously made goose stock and the port and cornstarch mixture.

To make the gravy, simmer the contents of the roasting pan on top of the stove for 1–2 minutes, scraping up any bits that are stuck and the coagulated roasting juices. Strain the liquid through a fine mesh strainer into a saucepan, pressing the juices out of the vegetables. Simmer several minutes, skimming the fat off the surface. Taste for seasoning and pour into a gravy boat.

Present the goose on a platter, surrounded by sage and rosemary sprigs. Carve the goose and serve it with a generous spoonful of stuffing and a dollop of gravy. Pass around your favorite jelly, such as cranberry or red currant.

Sausage and Sage Cornbread Stuffing

> 1 cup (240 mL) all purpose flour
> 1 Tbsp. (15 mL) baking powder
> 1 cup (240 mL) cornmeal
> ½ cup (120 mL) melted butter or margarine
> 1 cup (240 mL) buttermilk
> 1 egg
> 1 tsp. (5 mL) fresh sage, chopped
> Freshly ground black pepper, to taste
> ½ cup (120 mL) raisins or dried cranberries
> ¼ cup (60 mL) dry sherry
> 4 Tbsp. (60 mL) butter
> 1 cup (240 mL) diced shallots or onions
> 3 cloves garlic, finely chopped
> 1 lb. (455 g) sausage meat
> 1 Tbsp. (15 mL) chopped fresh sage, or 1 tsp. (5 mL) dried sage
> 3 Tbsp. (45 mL) chopped parsley
> 1 tsp. (5 mL) fresh lemon thyme, or ½ tsp. (2.5 mL) dried thyme
> 1 egg, beaten

To make the cornbread for the stuffing:

Preheat the oven to 375°F (190°C).

Grease 2 8-inch (20-cm) pans. Mix the flour, baking powder and cornmeal. In another bowl, mix the butter, buttermilk and egg. Stir the liquid mixture into the dry ingredients. Stir in the sage and pepper. Pour the batter into the pans. [Note: If you are using the recipe to make cornbread for another occasion, bake it in one 8-inch (20-cm) pan for 20 minutes.] Bake for 10–15 minutes. When cool, crumble 4 cups (950 mL) of the cornbread for the stuffing

To make the stuffing:

Soak the raisins or cranberries in the sherry for 1 hour.

Melt 2 Tbsp. (30 mL) of the butter in a large frying pan, and sauté the shallots or onion and garlic until limp. Melt the remaining butter in the frying pan, add the crumbled sausage meat, and brown. Add 4 cups (950 mL) of crumbled cornbread, the raisins or cranberries in sherry, sage, parsley and thyme. Stir gently, mix in the egg, and set aside.

Sicilian Sweet and Sour Pumpkin with Fresh Mint

About 10 years ago I took an Italian Cordon Bleu course with a teacher who was visiting from Rome. This recipe for Zucca Gialia in Agro-Dolce, which I learned in one of the classes, became a favorite, and I've been making it ever since.

Serves 10

> ½ cup (120 mL) olive oil
> 2 lb. (900 g) pumpkin, peeled and cut into ¼- to ½-inch
> (.6- to1.2-cm) strips
> Salt and freshly ground black pepper, to taste
> 5 cloves garlic, crushed
> 1 Tbsp. (15 mL) sugar, dissolved in ½ cup (120 mL) red wine vinegar
> 25 fresh mint leaves, or 2 tsp. (10 mL) dried mint

Heat the olive oil in a large frying pan over medium-high heat. Add 1 layer of pumpkin slices and brown on both sides. Add salt and pepper while frying. Drain on paper towel. Continue to sauté the pumpkin strips until they are all browned.

Arrange the pumpkin in a serving dish in layers. Reduce the heat to medium, add the garlic to the olive oil in the pan and sauté until lightly golden. Add the sugared vinegar and simmer for 2–3 minutes. Add the mint and remove from the heat.

Pour the sauce over the pumpkin, and allow to marinate for 3–4 hours, or overnight. Serve at room temperature, garnished with mint leaves. If you don't have fresh mint, garnish the dish with fresh Italian flat-leaf parsley.

Red Cabbage with Red Wine, Bay Leaves and Thyme

Red cabbage is a traditional accompaniment to goose.

Serves 6–8

    4 lb. (1.8 kg) red cabbage, thinly sliced
    2 cups (475 mL) chicken stock
    1 cup (240 mL) robust red wine
    2 bay leaves
    1 Tbsp. (15 mL) fresh thyme leaves
    2 cloves garlic
    Salt and freshly ground black pepper, to taste

Combine all the ingredients in a large frying pan with a lid. Cover and simmer for approximately 20 minutes, stirring occasionally, until the cabbage is tender. Remove the bay leaves, season to taste and serve hot.

Winter Squash

Winter varieties are easily grown and stored. While a dry, cool place is best for storage, not many people are successful at keeping a cool place dry. It is preferable to store squash at room temperature than somwhere cold and damp. Storage is helped by retaining the lower stem on the squash and wiping the fruit with a 10% solution of household bleach.

This slow-growing relative of celery needs a rich, moist soil and a long time in the ground. Start seedlings in February at house temperatures, move the plants to a cool greenhouse or cold frame on germination, and plant out in late April or May. Water well in dry periods, cover with 6 inches (15 cm) of sawdust before a severe frost, and consume in the darkest months.

Potato Celeriac Purée

I like to keep this simple, to allow the distinct flavor of the celeriac (celery root) to come through.

Serves 6–8

> 3 lb. (1.35 kg) red or russet potatoes, peeled and cut into chunks
> 1 medium-large celery root, peeled and cut into 1-inch (2.5-cm) dice
> ¼ lb. (113 g) butter
> ¼ cup (60 mL) finely chopped parsley
> 1 Tbsp. (15 mL) lemon juice
> ⅔–1 cup (160–240 mL) warm milk or cream
> Salt and freshly ground black pepper, to taste

Place the potatoes in a large pot, cover with water, add a pinch of salt, bring to a boil and cook until very tender, approximately 20 minutes. Drain and set aside.

Put the celery root and butter in a saucepan with just enough water to barely cover. Cover and cook over medium-low heat, adding more water if necessary, for 20–25 minutes, until the celeriac is tender. Stir occasionally.

Mash the potatoes, celeriac, parsley and lemon juice. Add the warm milk or cream, a little at a time, until you have the desired consistency. Season with salt and pepper.

Spinach and Swiss Chard Bundles

A charming way to present greens.

Serves 6–8

>2 bunches fresh spinach
>2 bunches Swiss chard
>2 Tbsp. (30 mL) butter
>2 shallots, finely chopped
>Salt and freshly ground black pepper, to taste

Wash the spinach and Swiss chard and remove any woody stems. Set aside about 12 of the larger spinach and chard leaves.

In a large pot, cook the rest of the spinach and Swiss chard with a little water and a pinch of salt, until it shrinks and is a fresh, bright green. Transfer to a large bowl and top with ice cubes or very cold water. Once cool, squeeze the excess water out and chop the greens coarsely.

Melt the butter in a large frying pan over medium-low heat. Add the shallots and sauté for 1 minute. Add the cooked spinach and Swiss chard. Season with salt and pepper and sauté for another 2–3 minutes until the greens are warm.

In a small saucepan, bring about 1 cup (240 mL) of salted water to a simmer. Quickly blanch the reserved leaves and lay them on a large platter. Divide the sautéed mixture between the leaves and roll each into a bundle. Brush with a little extra melted butter if desired. Serve immediately.

Pumpkin Chiffon Pie

A light and airy end to this Thanksgiving dinner. Agar-agar, a taste-less dried seaweed that is used as a setting agent, can be substituted for the gelatin in the pumpkin filling. Use about 1 tsp. (5 mL) in the same amount of water.

Serves 8

For the pastry:

> 1 cup (240 mL) unbleached all purpose flour
> ¼ cup (60 mL) sugar
> ½ tsp. (1.2 mL) ground cinnamon
> ½ tsp. (1.2 mL) salt
> ⅓ cup (80 mL) unsalted butter, cut into pieces
> 1 tsp. (5 mL) finely chopped lemon zest
> 1 Tbsp. (15 mL) fresh lemon juice

Preheat the oven to 375°F (190°C).

Combine the flour, sugar, cinnamon and salt together in a bowl. Using your fingertips or a pastry blender, cut in the butter until the mixture resembles coarse crumbs. Stir in the lemon zest and add just enough lemon juice to form a mass. Knead the dough gently into a ball, wrap in plastic wrap and refrigerate for 30 minutes.

Roll out the chilled dough on a lightly floured surface to form an 11-inch (28-cm) circle. Transfer to a 9-inch (23-cm) pie plate and press the dough into the bottom and sides. Trim the dough, leaving a 1-inch (2.5-cm) overhang. Fold the overhang back toward the inside, and crimp the edge decoratively. Prick the bottom of the pastry with a fork.

Line the pastry with parchment paper or aluminum foil with the shiny side down. Fill the pie plate with dried beans or pie weights and bake for 15 minutes.

Remove from the oven and reduce the heat to 350°F (175°C). Remove the foil and pie weights, and return the pie crust to the oven for another 15 minutes, or until golden brown. Remove from the oven and cool.

For the filling:

1 Tbsp. (15 mL) gelatin
¼ cup (60 mL) cold water
3 eggs, separated
½ cup (120 mL) sugar
1¼ cups (300 mL) canned pumpkin
½ cup (120 mL) milk
½ tsp. (2.5 mL) salt
½ tsp. (2.5 mL) cinnamon
½ tsp. (2.5 mL) nutmeg
¼ tsp. (1.2 mL) salt
½ cup (120 mL) sugar

Stir the gelatin into the cold water and set aside. Beat the 3 egg yolks slightly. Add ½ cup (120 mL) sugar, pumpkin, milk, ½ tsp. (2.5 mL) salt, cinnamon and nutmeg. Cook in a double boiler, stirring constantly, until thick. Stir in the soaked gelatin until it dissolves. Set aside to cool.

Whip the egg whites until stiff with the remaining ¼ tsp. (1.2 mL) salt. When the pumpkin mixture begins to set, stir in the remaining ½ cup (120 mL) sugar. Fold in the egg whites. Fill the pie shell and chill the pie for several hours before serving. Serve with lightly sweetened whipping cream.

November
and
December

Creating Light
in the Darkness

I like reality. It tastes of bread.

—Jean Anouilh

Perhaps the most vital gastronomic role at holiday gatherings is this: Without food, plenty of it, and lovingly prepared, we might kill one another.

—Bob Shacochis

There is grass on my chicken.

—Kyle Jackson, my six-year-old great-nephew,
referring to the carefully sprinkled dill

There are green specks in everything.

—Jenny Cameron, age 15, during
her first year at Ravenhill

In my experience, clever food is not appreciated at Christmas. It makes the little ones cry and the old ones nervous.

—Oliver Wendell Holmes, Sr.

As observant as I try to be, November always catches me by surprise. When did it start getting so dark in the morning? Where did the golden light of Indian summer go? When did we stop eating meals outside, or at least with the French doors open? Everything is changing—the light, the weather, the temperature and my behavior. I start rooting around in baskets for winter clothes (my whole life is stored in baskets) and think of things to warm us: shawls, sweaters, soup, fires in the evening, friends, rich stews, red for visual warmth, and celebrations to counteract the gloom. Banding together to eat and drink is tribal behavior that humans have always needed and enjoyed, and winter gatherings seem more intense because of the cold and the darkness. Historically this is the time of year that people will get ill or die, and I still take remedies such as vitamins and herbs to protect myself from illness.

Sometimes we go away in October when it still feels warm and sunny, and when we return in November the season has changed. The brilliant golden maple leaves that were clinging on in October now litter the driveway in a wash of color. The brown oak leaves fall and the raking of leaves begins. They are piled into the leaf mold pen to rot away in the rain all winter long. In spring the lovely, rotted, rich mulch is spread all over the garden and nature's cycle of nourishment begins again.

I often wake early in the morning when it is still very dark and make tea and let the dogs loose. I peer out the door into the darkness, and if I am lucky, I hear the owls calling from the old Douglas fir trees. These great horned owls live up and down the mountainside behind the farm. The sight and sound of owls is a profound experience. It makes me realize why these creatures appear in so many tales and legends, especially in children's books.

Andrew is busy tidying up the garden, and sowing fall rye in empty raised beds for green manure. In the spring he cuts off the green grass and composts it, turning under the roots of the rye grass. This adds rich organic material to the beds and also stops the soil from being washed down the hill. The garlic and shallots have been planted for next summer's harvest; their little yellow tips poke through the earth in soldierly rows. Broad beans are also planted and, barring a really bad frost, this gives the gardener a jump-start in the spring. Winter-planted beans are ready to eat much earlier and avoid the wicked aphid attacks that come with the warmer weather.

The highlight of November is our annual craft fair at Ravenhill. It is always held on the last Sunday of the month. We have been organizing this event for over 10 years and it has become an institution. When we are very old it will probably still go on. I envision us sitting outside in twig chairs watching the people go into the barn.

The barn gets a big clean-out and Andrew does a location map for the placement of the artists' booths. We hang lights and boughs and get set up for playing Christmas music. My daughter Jenny and her husband David sell cookies, bagels and baked potatoes, which seem to be a good food for a crisp

November day. They fire up the old woodstove and heat fresh apple juice that comes from a farm on Oldfield Road not far from us. People arrive at 10 o'clock. All the artists are local and there is a wide selection of craftspeople—potters, jewelers, angel makers, cheesemakers, heritage apple growers, knitters, wheat weavers, Christmas cake makers, wreath makers and hat makers, to mention a few. Some of the sheep and the goat and donkey are put in the barn to add to the Christmas stable atmosphere. Joker, the donkey, sometimes refuses to come in unless tempted by lots of carrots. This year we could place Nina, our new granddaughter, in with the animals to add an authentic touch but her mother might not approve.

There is a short respite after the craft fair, and then suddenly Christmas looms. When I think of Christmas the color red, surrounded by darkness, appears on my visual screen. One of the best Christmas scenes on film is in Ingmar Bergman's *Fanny and Alexander*. It is filled with the color red, flashing crystal glasses, music, laughter, luxury, candlelight and bawdy humor. It is my fantasy to create that atmosphere on Christmas Eve and wear a red velvet Victorian dress. Films and literature have always provided me with sources of inspiration for entertaining, be it a Christmas feast or a sensuous late August picnic redolent with basil and fresh-picked tomatoes still hot from the sun. In reality my fantasy meals often have imperfections, such as swarms of wasps or difficult guests, but I keep striving for perfection.

My favorite meal is the seafood buffet we prepare on Christmas Eve. It is simple and very elegant and easier on the cook, who has Christmas dinner to make the next day. It features fresh oysters, smoked salmon, scallops, caviar, oyster bisque, crab cakes, a dark rye bread and blinis, which are the most serious cooked item on the menu. The dinner has Russian and Scandinavian overtones and is served with champagne, which heightens the celebratory atmosphere.

I fill the house with candles, holly and green boughs. I even put green boughs on the ground outside the door, so guests can smell the scent of cedar and fir when boots crunch over them. Sometimes I hang the bare magnolia tree with my collection of lanterns lit with little tea-candle lights. They glow beautifully as guests arrive.

The day after Christmas, Boxing Day, is another favorite. It can be very relaxing, as the cold turkey is ready, waiting to be nibbled at. We often take walks through the valley and visit the old church and graveyard where the early pioneers, mostly from Scotland and England, proclaim the names of their birthplaces on their tombstones. This exercise helps counteract feelings of Christmas excess. We then return home and carve some more turkey, slathering it with cranberry sauce, and eat it in front of the fire with some good bread and wine.

The intense feelings Christmas inspires are a mixture of childhood memories, unrequited wishes, and longing for intimacy and warmth. I once read a description of an early 19th-century Christmas on a vast estate in Essex. Once a year the peasant farmers were given warm blankets, extra food and beer. Their excitement at this generosity, so rare the rest of the year and such a contrast to their daily life, was almost unbearable for them. It gave me an understanding of the tension and excitement that Christmas still creates in our lives.

The last menu that marks the closing of the year is a dinner "pour deux" for New Year's Eve. This is a charming contrast to loud noisy parties and chips and dip. Planning a special meal for just two means the menu can be excessive. Set a beautiful table with your prettiest dishes, flowers, candles and silver. Buy some very good wine, and two tender, plump beef fillets. The carrot soup has an orange flavor, there is a fennel potato gratin, and for dessert a comfy, tart, lemon and lavender bread pudding, a perfect finale for an intimate dinner. The theme of this dinner is citrus flavors and the licorice taste of fennel, all of which brighten the eaters' palates, and hopefully their spirits too. Toast each other and the coming New Year.

We have come to the end of the year, the end of our menus, and the end of this book. I hope the book warms you, entertains you and nourishes you. After more than 40 years of cooking for myself and others I have learned two wonderful lessons: food that is shared with friends and family tastes better than food eaten alone; and growing and cooking your own food from the garden is one of life's richest and healthiest pleasures.

Idyllic Italian Dinner

Italian cuisine suits life at Ravenhill. Simple, straightforward flavors, immediacy of taste and a passion for vegetables and herbs marry well with a gardener's spirit.

Lentil and Sorrel Soup

*Spinach Tagliatelle with Grilled Scallops
and Roast Red Pepper Sauce*

Lemon Zucchini alla Pancetta

Calamari Stufati alla Marinara
(Stuffed Squid in Marinara Sauce)

Pumpkin Ginger Soufflé

Lentil and Sorrel Soup

I love any kind of lentil soup. I adapted this one from a soup served at the famous River Cafe in London, England.

Serves 6

> 1¼ cups (300 mL) green lentils
> 1 clove garlic, unpeeled
> 1 bay leaf
> 1 sprig sage
> ¼ cup (60 mL) butter
> 2 Tbsp. (30 mL) olive oil
> 2 shallots or 1 small red onion, finely chopped
> 2 cloves garlic, peeled
> 2¼ lb. (1 kg) fresh sorrel, stems removed, thinly sliced
> 2½ cups (600 mL) hot chicken stock
> 10 oz. (285 g) spinach leaves, thinly sliced
> Salt and freshly ground black pepper, to taste
> ½ cup (120 mL) Crème Fraîche (page 146)
> ½ cup (120 mL) freshly grated Parmesan cheese

Place the lentils, unpeeled garlic, bay leaf and sage in a saucepan with cold water to cover. Bring to a boil and simmer for about 25 minutes, or until the lentils are tender.

Melt the butter with the olive oil in a large saucepan over medium-low heat. Sauté the shallots or onion and peeled garlic cloves until soft, approximately 8–10 minutes. Add half the sorrel and cook for 2 minutes until it has wilted. Stir in ¾ of the lentils and half the chicken stock.

Transfer to a food processor and process until smooth. You may have to process it in 2 batches. Add the uncooked sorrel and pulse a few times. Return the mixture to the large saucepan and add the remaining lentils, the spinach and the rest of the chicken stock. Season with salt and pepper. Heat gently and serve with crème fraîche and Parmesan cheese on the side.

Spinach Tagliatelle with Grilled Scallops and Roast Red Pepper Sauce

This dish was a favorite of a couple I cooked for when I first started cooking privately in Vancouver. It is delicious, low fat and has a lovely presentation. Tagliatelle is the northern Italian name for fettuccine.

Serves 4–6

> 4–5 medium red bell peppers
> Juice and zest of 1 lemon
> ½ cup (120 mL) fresh dill or favorite fresh herb in season
> (such as fennel, tarragon, Italian parsley)
> Salt and freshly ground black pepper, to taste
> 1–1½ lb. (455–680 g) fresh spinach tagliatelle, or other spinach pasta
> 2 Tbsp. (30 mL) olive oil
> 1 bunch spinach, cooked, squeezed of excess water, and
> coarsely chopped
> 24–28 fresh, plump white scallops

Slice the red peppers in half lengthwise and remove the core and seeds. Place cut side down on a lightly oiled baking sheet and broil them until the skin is blistered and black, about 5 minutes. Remove from the oven and place the peppers in a plastic bag for about 10 minutes. Remove from the bag and peel off the skin.

Place the peppers, lemon juice and zest, herbs, salt and pepper in a food processor. Blend until smooth.

Bring a large pot of salted water to a boil. Cook the pasta until al dente, about 5 minutes. Drain and toss with the olive oil, spinach and roast pepper sauce.

Meanwhile, heat a lightly oiled grill pan or barbecue to very hot. Grill the scallops about 1 minute per side. Place them on top of the tossed pasta, season with salt and pepper and serve.

Lemon Zucchini alla Pancetta

Green vegetables add nutrition and plate appeal to a meal. This dish is quick and easy to make and very tasty.

Serves 4–6

> ¼ cup (60 mL) olive oil
> 4 oz. (113 g) pancetta or prosciutto, cut into small pieces
> 1 medium red onion, thinly sliced
> 3 cloves garlic, finely chopped
> 6 small zucchini, cut into ½ inch (1.2 cm) rounds
> Juice of 1 lemon
> Salt and freshly ground black pepper
> ½ cup (120 mL) chopped Italian parsley
> 1 Tbsp. (15 mL) capers (optional)

Heat the olive oil in a large frying pan over medium heat. Add the pancetta or prosciutto and the onion and cook for about 10 minutes, until the onion is translucent. Add the garlic and sauté for a few more minutes. Add the zucchini and half the lemon juice. Season with salt and pepper.

Cook for another 10 minutes, until the zucchini is tender but still firm. Add the rest of the lemon juice and the parsley.

Transfer to a serving dish, sprinkle with more freshly ground pepper and capers, if desired, and serve immediately.

Calamari Stufati alla Marinara
(Stuffed Squid in Marinara Sauce)

Deep frying is not the only way to prepare this wonderful seafood. Here, rich flavors complement the simply prepared squid. Serve it on its own or with your favorite pasta.

Serves 4–6

To stuff the squid:

½ lb. (225 g) mixed mushrooms, finely chopped
1–2 Tbsp. (15–30 mL) extra virgin olive oil
2 Tbsp. (30 mL) finely chopped tarragon
2 cloves garlic, finely chopped
1 egg, lightly beaten
2 Tbsp. (30 mL) freshly grated Parmesan cheese
¼ cup (60 mL) fine dry bread crumbs
Salt and freshly ground black pepper, to taste
4–6 large squid, 4–5 inches long (10–12.5 cm), cleaned and
   left whole

Combine all the ingredients except the squid and mix well. If the mixture is too dry, add a little more olive oil. If it is too wet, add a little more Parmesan cheese or bread crumbs. The stuffing should hold together when you squeeze it in your hand.

Spoon the stuffing into the squid sacs, being careful not to over-stuff. Set aside.

To make the marinara sauce:

 2 Tbsp. (30 mL) olive oil
 4 cloves garlic, finely chopped
 ½ cup (120 mL) red wine
 1 28-oz. (796-mL) can Italian plum tomatoes, puréed, or
 1 lb. (455 g) fresh tomatoes, finely chopped
 Salt and freshly ground black pepper, to taste
 2 sprigs fresh basil
 ½ cup (120 mL) chopped fresh parsley

Heat the olive oil over medium-low heat and sauté the garlic until it is
a pale blond color. Add the wine and simmer for 1 minute. Add the
tomatoes, salt, pepper and basil, and simmer for approximately
30 minutes, until the sauce is smooth and somewhat thick. Stir in
the parsley and taste for seasoning.

To assemble the dish:

Heat 2 Tbsp. (30 mL) olive oil in a large frying pan. Place the squid in
the pan and brown each side lightly.

Add the marinara sauce, cover and cook for another 15 minutes.
Check the squid for tenderness by pricking with a fork. The squid
should be firm, but not rubbery. Cook a little longer if necessary.

Pumpkin Ginger Soufflé

Pumpkin is incredibly versatile and this dessert is a perfect finish.

Serves 6

> 1 cup (240 mL) cooked pumpkin purée
> ¼ cup (60 mL) maple syrup
> ¼ tsp. (1.2 mL) nutmeg
> ¼ tsp. (1.2 mL) ginger
> ⅛ tsp. (.5 mL) salt
> 2 Tbsp. (30 mL) butter
> 6 eggs, separated
> 3 Tbsp. (45 mL) brown sugar
> ½ cup (120 mL) granulated sugar

Preheat the oven to 350°F (180°C).

In a saucepan, combine the pumpkin purée, maple syrup, nutmeg, ginger, salt and butter. Stir over low heat for 5 minutes. Beat the egg yolks and add them slowly, while stirring, to the pumpkin mixture. Heat through gently, taking care not to curdle the eggs.

In a separate bowl, beat the egg whites until they form stiff peaks. Fold the egg whites and brown sugar gently into the pumpkin mixture.

Grease a 4-cup (1-L) soufflé dish, sprinkle it with granulated sugar and pour in the pumpkin mixture. Bake for about 30 minutes, until the soufflé is puffed and golden on top. Serve immediately.

Christmas Eve Seafood Extravaganza

The night before Christmas you may want a celebratory supper, but not one that is too complicated. Our family has been seduced by the Norwegian and Italian custom of serving a smorgasbord where seafood predominates. We have three birthdays to celebrate within the week before Christmas, including one on Christmas Eve, so the festivities start early. Here is a menu that requires more shopping than cooking, so you can relax and graze, sip champagne, and laugh with those nearest and dearest. Enjoy it with a little iced Russian vodka to warm your soul.

Fresh Oysters on the Half Shell with Mignonette Sauce

Quick Oyster Soup

Stir-fried Scallops with Green Onion and Cilantro

Vodka Lime Prawns

Smoked Salmon with Russian Blinis, Sour Cream and Caviar

Pezzetti Fritti of Broccoli, Artichokes and Zucchini

Chocolate-Dipped Mandarin Oranges

Fresh Oysters on the Half Shell with Mignonette Sauce

Buy some fresh local oysters in the shell—not too large, as the small, plump ones are sweeter. Allow 2–3 per person (plus 1 per person for the oyster soup). Order the oysters at least a week ahead of time to ensure your fishmonger has them.

Shuck the oysters, severing the muscle that attaches the oyster to the shell, and remove any bits of shell left behind. Present the oysters on a deep serving platter lined with an abundance of rosemary or other greenery. Leave a space in the middle for a small bowl of mignonette sauce. If you are serving a lot of oysters, put ice under the greens.

Mignonette Sauce

Makes 1 cup (240 mL)

> 1 cup (240 mL) tarragon vinegar
> 2 shallots or one small red onion, finely chopped
> ½ tsp. (2.5 mL) finely chopped lemon zest
> ½ tsp. (2.5 mL) sea salt
> ½ tsp. (2.5 mL) hot pepper sauce
> Freshly ground black pepper, to taste

Combine all the ingredients and refrigerate until ready to use. Let your guests spoon a little mignonette sauce on their own oysters—some purists like to slurp their oysters *au naturel*.

Quick Oyster Soup

Brothy and comforting. Because this menu has an abundance of seafood, the soup servings are small. Double the recipe for oyster fans.

Serves 8

8 fresh oysters, shucked and reserved in their own liquor

4 cups (950 mL) milk

½ cup (120 mL) champagne or white wine

1 Tbsp. (15 mL) butter

1 bay leaf

1 shallot finely chopped

1 clove garlic, finely chopped

Sea salt and freshly ground pepper, to taste

¼ cup (60 mL) finely chopped fresh Italian parsley

½ tsp. (2.5 mL) paprika

In a heavy saucepan combine the milk, champagne or wine, butter, bay leaf, shallot, garlic, salt and pepper. Bring to a gentle simmer over medium-low heat. Add the oysters and their liquor, and return the soup to a simmer. Cook for 1 minute longer.

Add the parsley and paprika, taste for seasoning and serve in small bowls, placing one oyster in each bowl.

Welsh Onion

It may not be a native of Wales, and it isn't much like an onion, but its stout, tubular leaves have a strong chive flavor, and the plant rarely disappears in cold winters. The clusters of bulbs need dividing every two or three years. The plant survives dry soil in summer and needs little fertilizer.

Scallops cook quickly, so be careful not to over-cook them.

Serves 6

¼ cup (60 mL) sherry
1 Tbsp. (15 mL) soy sauce
1 Tbsp. (15 mL) rice wine vinegar
1 tsp. (5 mL) cornstarch
2 Tbsp. (30 mL) olive oil
1 lb. (455 g) plump, white scallops, well drained
1 bunch green onions, or Welsh onion, finely chopped
1 bunch cilantro, big stems removed, finely chopped
Salt and freshly ground black pepper, to taste
1 tsp. (5 mL) sesame oil

Combine the sherry, soy sauce, vinegar and corn-starch in a small bowl and mix well. Set aside.

Heat a large frying pan or wok over medium heat. When the pan is quite hot, add the olive oil. Add the scallops and sear for 2 minutes, tossing several times. Toss the onion and cilantro with the scallops and cook for 1 minute more. Add the sherry mixture and toss the scallops again. Cook for 1 minute more. The scallops are done when they become opaque.

Season with salt and pepper, place on a platter or in a shallow bowl and drizzle with the sesame oil.

Vodka Lime Prawns

When I worked at Delilah's, a Vancouver restaurant, I made a similar dish with tequila.

Serves 4–6

   ¼ lb. (113 g) butter
   2 cloves garlic, finely chopped
   1 tsp. (5 mL) finely chopped fresh sage
   ½ tsp. (2.5 mL) ground cumin
   ½ tsp. (2.5 mL) fennel seed
   1 lb. (455 g) medium prawns, peeled, tail left on
   ⅛ cup (30 mL) good-quality vodka
   Juice of 2 small limes
   Salt and freshly ground black pepper, to taste

Heat a large frying pan or wok over medium heat. Melt the butter, then add the garlic, sage, cumin, fennel seed and prawns. Cook for 2–3 minutes, tossing several times, until the prawns are just pink.

Turn the heat up slightly and add the vodka and lime juice. Let it bubble for 1 minute and season with salt and pepper. Serve on a platter or in a shallow bowl.

Smoked Salmon with Russian Blinis, Sour Cream and Caviar

Any leftovers are great with bagels and cream cheese or in a fluffy omelet. A side of pre-sliced smoked salmon weighs 1–2 lb. (455–900 g). When choosing caviar, lumpfish is the most common and inexpensive type and can be found in most supermarket seafood departments.

Serves 8–10 generously

> Winter greens, such as kale, arugula, mustard greens or frisée
> 1 cup (240 mL) sour cream
> ¼ cup (60 mL) capers or caperberries
> 1 2-oz. (57-g) jar red caviar
> 1 2-oz. (57-g) jar black caviar
> 1 recipe Russian Blinis
> 1½ lb. (680 g) smoked salmon, approximately
> 2 lemons, cut into 8 wedges

Arrange a large platter with the winter greens. Place the sour cream, capers, and jars of caviar each in their own small bowls down the center. Place a serving spoon in each bowl. Create a layered arrangement of blinis on one side, and slices of smoked salmon on the other. Surround the salmon with lemon wedges.

Russian Blinis

There are many blini recipes; this is the one we use on Christmas Eve. It is a classical blini recipe, given to us by an old Jewish friend. If you are using sage or rosemary instead of thyme, use only 1 tsp. (5 mL), as the flavor can be overpowering in such light, fluffy morsels. For buckwheat blinis, use half buckwheat and half all purpose white flour.

Makes about 4 dozen small blinis

  1¾ cup (420 mL) buttermilk

  1 tsp. (5 mL) sugar

  1 package, or 1 level Tbsp. (15 mL) active dry yeast

  1½ cups (360 mL) unbleached all purpose white flour

  ½ tsp. (2.5 mL) salt

  1 tsp. (5 mL) sugar

  3 Tbsp. (45 mL) unsalted butter, melted

  2 Tbsp. (30 mL) vegetable or olive oil, plus a little more for frying

  1 Tbsp. (15 mL) finely chopped fresh thyme, or other winter herbs,
      such as rosemary, sage or parsley

  3 large egg yolks

  2 large egg whites

Bring the buttermilk to a simmer in a small saucepan over medium-low
heat. Transfer to a large bowl and cool to lukewarm, approximately
105–115°F (40.5–46°C). Add 1 tsp. (5 mL) sugar and the yeast to the
milk, stir and let stand until foamy, about 5–10 minutes.

Whisk in the flour, salt, remaining sugar, butter, 2 Tbsp. (30 mL)
oil, fresh herbs and egg yolks until smooth. Cover and let rise in a
warm place until doubled in size, about 1 hour.

In a separate bowl, beat the egg whites until they form stiff peaks.
Fold them into the batter. Rub a large non-stick or well-seasoned
frying pan with a little oil and heat for 1 minute over medium heat.
Drop the batter into the pan, 1 Tbsp. (15 mL) at a time, spacing the
mounds about 1 inch (2.5 cm) apart. Cook until the underside is
golden, about 1 minute. Flip over and cook 30 seconds more. Transfer
to a heat-resistant plate. Repeat with the remaining batter, greasing
the skillet between each batch. Keep the cooked blinis warm by
covering them with aluminum foil in a 275°F (135°C) oven.

Pezzetti Fritti of Broccoli, Artichokes and Zucchini

This is my own version of the traditional Italian Christmas Eve dish called pezzetti, which means "small pieces."

Serves 8–10

> 2 heads broccoli, approximately 3 lb. (1.35 kg), cut into small florets
> 2–3 eggs
> 3 cups (720 mL) fine bread crumbs, toasted
> 1 cup (240 mL) Parmesan cheese
> 1 Tbsp. (15 mL) finely chopped winter savory
> 1–2 medium zucchinis, approximately 1½ lb. (680 g), quartered and cut into pieces similar in size to the florets
> 2 14-oz. (398-mL) cans small whole artichoke hearts, approximately 10–12, well-drained
> ½ cup (120 mL) olive oil
> Salt and freshly ground black pepper, to taste
> 2 Tbsp. (30 mL) finely chopped Italian parsley

Blanch the broccoli florets in a large pot of simmering salted water for 1–2 minutes, until barely tender. Remove them with a slotted spoon and plunge into a bowl of cold water. Drain well and set aside.

In a small bowl, beat the eggs lightly. Combine the bread crumbs, Parmesan cheese and winter savory and spread on a plate. Dip the broccoli, one piece at a time, into the beaten eggs, allowing the excess egg to flow back into the bowl. Dredge the florets in the bread-crumb mixture, patting it lightly with your fingertips to make sure the florets are firmly breaded. Set them aside. Repeat the process with the zucchini and artichoke hearts.

Heat the oil in a large frying pan over medium-high heat. When hot, slip in as many broccoli pieces as will fit loosely in a single layer. When they have formed a nice golden crust on one side, turn and cook the other side. When they are done on both sides, transfer them to paper towels and season with salt and pepper. Repeat with the remaining vegetables. Toss them with the parsley and serve warm.

Chocolate-Dipped Mandarin Oranges

The bittersweet chocolate combines perfectly with the pow of the mandarin juice.

Makes 70—80 chocolates

> 1 lb. (455 g) high-quality bittersweet chocolate, such as Callebaut
> 10 mandarin oranges, peeled, sectioned, pith removed, and
>   wrapped in a clean, damp cloth

Line 1 or 2 cookie sheets with parchment paper or aluminum foil. Melt the chocolate in the top of a double boiler over hot, not simmering, water. Remove the double boiler top from the heat. Pick up the fruit with a toothpick, dip it in the chocolate, and swirl it gently to coat it. Let the excess drip off. Lay the mandarin segment on the cookie sheet (you can leave the toothpick in for serving or remove it). Repeat with the remaining segments. Place the chocolate-covered fruit in the refrigerator, or a cool place, to harden and set the chocolate.

Arrange the segments on an attractive platter. For an interesting presentation, spear each chocolate with a decorative toothpick and insert into half a cantaloupe, placed on a plate cut side down.

New Year's Eve Dinner
for Your Sweetie

Two's a party, three's a crowd. Set the tone for the evening with candles, wine and music. It would be romantic to begin this intimate evening by preparing the dinner together.

Hot Herbaceous Crab Dip

Grilled Fillet of Beef in a Black Currant Sauce

Broiled Mushrooms

Tomato Leek Provençal

Fennel and Potato Gratin

Lemon Lavender Bread Pudding

Hot Herbaceous Crab Dip

A warm and creamy beginning for a memorable evening. For a larger group, double the ingredients. Serve with crackers, tortilla chips or slices of baguette.

Makes approximately 2 cups (475 mL)

1 Tbsp. (15 mL) melted butter
⅓ cup (80 mL) bread crumbs
½ lb. (225 g) fresh crabmeat
¼ cup (60 mL) finely chopped celery
⅛ cup (30 mL) finely chopped red bell pepper
1 shallot, finely chopped
1 green onion, finely chopped
2 tsp. (10 mL) fresh lemon juice
¼ tsp. (1.2 mL) sea salt
2 Tbsp. (30 mL) soft cream cheese
¼ cup (60 mL) mayonnaise
1 tsp. (5 mL) Dijon mustard
Hot pepper sauce, to taste
1 Tbsp. (15 mL) finely chopped Italian parsley, half reserved
    for garnish
½ tsp. (2.5 mL) finely chopped fresh rosemary

Preheat the oven to 350°F (175°C).

Combine the melted butter and bread crumbs. In a separate bowl combine all the other ingredients. Place the mixture in a small, lightly buttered gratin dish or medium soufflé dish. Top with the bread crumb mixture and bake in a preheated oven for approximately 10 minutes, until it's bubbling.

Grilled Fillet of Beef in a Black Currant Sauce

I was privileged to assist Jacques Pepin in 1994 and I fell in love with his venison in black currant sauce. Since then I have created my own version, which is a little more "herby" and garlicky, with just a hint of sweetness. The original recipe was sweeter, with a demi-glace, which is a reduced brown stock. Beef fillet has a more delicate flavor than venison, so a lighter sauce is called for. The recipe makes approximately 1 cup (240 mL) of sauce.

Serves 2

> 2 6- to 8-oz. (170- to 225-g) beef fillets
> 1 tsp. (5 mL) finely chopped fresh rosemary
> Freshly ground black pepper
> 1 Tbsp. (15 mL) unbleached white flour
> 1 Tbsp. (15 mL) each olive oil and butter
> 2 shallots, finely chopped
> 2 cloves garlic, finely chopped
> 1 cup (240 mL) robust red wine or port
> 1 tsp. (5 mL) red wine vinegar
> 1 Tbsp. (15 mL) black currant jelly, or more if you prefer it sweeter
> Salt and freshly ground black pepper, to taste
> 1–2 Tbsp. (15–30 mL) water or stock, if necessary

Rub the fillets in the rosemary, pepper and flour.

Heat a well-seasoned grill pan or cast-iron pan over medium heat. When the pan is quite hot, add the olive oil and swirl it around to coat the pan. Cook the fillets for 4–5 minutes per side, depending on the thickness, to produce a medium-rare fillet. Remove from the pan, place on a warm plate and cover with foil.

Melt the butter in the same pan and sauté the shallots and garlic for 1 minute. Add the wine or port, vinegar and jelly, scraping up any bits that have stuck to the bottom of the pan and incorporating them into the sauce. Season with salt and pepper and add a little water or stock if necessary. Place the fillets—and any juices that have emerged—back in the pan. Coat the fillets with the sauce and serve with extra sauce on top.

Broiled Mushrooms

If you wish, you can cook the mushrooms before you cook the steaks and keep them warm.

Serves 2

> 2 large portobello mushrooms, or any favorite mushrooms,
>   such as oyster, chanterelle or porcini
> 1 Tbsp. (15 mL) lemon juice
> 1 clove garlic, finely chopped or pressed
> 1 tsp. (5 mL) finely chopped fresh sage
> 1 Tbsp. (15 mL) olive oil
> Salt and freshly ground black pepper, to taste

Combine all the ingredients in a small bowl. Heat a well-seasoned cast-iron pan or grill pan over medium heat. Cook the mushrooms about 2–3 minutes per side. Remove and keep warm until serving time.

Tomato Leek Provençal

This is a traditional French accompaniment for beef fillet.

Serves 2

    2½ Tbsp. (37.5 mL) extra virgin olive oil
    ½ medium leek, cleaned well and finely chopped
    2 medium tomatoes, ripe but not too soft
    2 cloves garlic, finely chopped
    ¼ cup (60 mL) finely chopped fresh parsley
    2 Tbsp. (30 mL) bread crumbs
    Salt and freshly ground black pepper, to taste

Turn the oven to broil and place a rack in the center of the oven.

In a medium frying pan, heat 2 Tbsp. (30 mL) of the olive oil. Add the leek and sauté until it's wilted, approximately 3 minutes. Set aside.

To make a crowned tomato, pierce it with a sharp paring knife about ¾ inch (2 cm) down from the stem end of the tomato. Cut around the top of the tomato in a zigzag pattern to make the crowned effect. Gently twist the tomato to remove the top.

In a small bowl, mix the garlic, parsley, leeks, bread crumbs, salt and pepper. Place the tomatoes in a lightly oiled baking pan or cookie sheet. Top each tomato generously with the mixture, patting it down. Drizzle the remaining olive oil on the tomatoes. Place the baking pan on the oven rack so the tomatoes are not directly under the broiler, and broil them until they are tender and the tops are golden brown. Serve immediately.

Fennel and Potato Gratin

A nourishing, creamy indulgence.

Serves 2–4

> 1 Tbsp. (15 mL) olive oil
> 1 large fennel bulb, quartered lengthwise, cored and thinly sliced,
>   approximately 2 cups (475 mL)
> ¾ lb. (340 g) potatoes, thinly sliced just prior to baking
> 3 cloves garlic, finely chopped
> ½ cup (120 mL) white wine or dry white vermouth
> 2 Tbsp. (30 mL) freshly chopped herbs, such as Italian parsley
>   or thyme
> 1 recipe Béchamel Sauce (see page 192)
> ½ cup (120 mL) freshly grated Parmesan cheese

Preheat the oven to 375°F (190°C).

Heat a frying pan over medium heat. Add the olive oil, fennel, potatoes and garlic. Sauté for 2–3 minutes. Add the wine or vermouth and reduce the heat to low. Cover the pan and steam for approximately 5 minutes. Transfer the fennel and potato mixture to a bowl and toss with half the fresh herbs.

Place the vegetables evenly in a lightly buttered gratin dish. Pour the Béchamel Sauce evenly on top and sprinkle with the Parmesan cheese. Bake uncovered for 15–20 minutes, until the vegetables are tender and the top is golden. Remove from the oven, sprinkle with the remaining herbs, and allow to sit for 5 minutes before serving.

Béchamel Sauce

Makes 2 cups (475 mL)

> 2 Tbsp. (30 mL) butter
> 1 Tbsp. (15 mL) unbleached white flour
> ⅛ tsp. (.5 mL) nutmeg
> Salt and freshly ground black pepper, to taste
> 2 cups (475 mL) milk, approximately
> 1 bay leaf

Melt the butter over medium heat in a medium, heavy saucepan. Add the flour, nutmeg, salt and pepper. Cook for 1–2 minutes, stirring occasionally.

Add the milk a little at a time, whisking constantly until smooth. When the mixture begins to thicken, add the bay leaf. Continue whisking in the milk until the mixture becomes a smooth, velvety sauce. It shouldn't be too thick. When it begins to simmer, it is at its maximum thickness. Add a little more milk if necessary. Simmer gently for 2 minutes more, remove the pan from the heat and take out the bay leaf.

Lemon Lavender Bread Pudding

In winter, when there are no lavender flowers, I like to cook with the leaves. It gives me a lift to taste that summery essence in winter.

Serves 2–4

2 cups (475 mL) milk

1 cup (240 mL) cream

¼ tsp. (1.2 mL) salt

4–5 lavender leaves

1 tsp. (5 mL) finely chopped lemon zest

3½ cups (840 mL) white bread, cut into cubes and toasted

3 eggs, separated

⅓ cup (80 mL) brown sugar

1 tsp. (5 mL) vanilla

½ tsp. (2.5 mL) cinnamon

3 Tbsp. (45 mL) fresh lemon juice

½ cup (120 mL) dried cranberries (optional)

1 Tbsp. (15 mL) brown sugar for topping

Preheat the oven to 350°F (175°C).

Heat the milk, cream, salt, lavender leaves and lemon zest until almost simmering. Let steep for 5 minutes. Pour the mixture through a fine mesh strainer over the bread and let soak for 15 minutes.

Beat together the egg yolks, ⅓ cup (80 mL) sugar, vanilla, cinnamon and lemon juice. Add the cranberries, if desired, and stir the mixture into the bread and milk. Beat the egg whites until stiff and fold them in.

Pour into a greased 8-inch (20-cm) square baking dish or a medium soufflé dish. Sprinkle the top of the pudding with the remaining sugar. Place the dish in a larger pan. Pour hot water into the larger pan; it should come ¼ of the way up the sides of the soufflé dish. Bake for approximately 45 minutes, or until the pudding is set. Check the water level after 20 minutes, and add more water if necessary.

Index

About the Authors

PHOTO BY DAVID CRONE

Noël Richardson and her daughter, Jenny Cameron, were using herbs in their day-to-day life long before it became a popular trend in health care and cookery.

Noël makes her home at Ravenhill Farm on Vancouver Island, one of the most well-known working herb farms in British Columbia. Since starting the farm with her husband Andrew Yeoman in 1979, Noël and Andrew have transformed it into the heart of a lifestyle and career based on the use of herbs. Writing cookbooks, restaurant reviewing and food writing for *Western Living* and *City Food Magazine* and teaching cooking classes in the kitchen of Ravenhill Farm prompted the creation of Noël's three earlier best-selling books, *Winter Pleasures, Summer Delights* and *In a Country Garden*.

Jenny inherited her mother's love for herbs and cooking. Travelling extensively in Europe allowed her to experience a variety of cultures and foods. Like her mother, Jenny transformed her passion for herbs and cooking into a career. She holds a professional diploma from the Dubrulle Culinary School, and has been a professional caterer and cooking instructor for 12 years. She makes her home with her husband David and young daughter Nina at Ravenhill Farm, where they are caretakers and gardeners.

Many of the recipes in *Herbal Celebrations* are favorites that both mother and daughter have enjoyed together.